PRAISE FOR
BORN TO BUZZ

"We deserve life experiences that truly fulfill us, yet we all know that feeling that something is missing as we juggle careers, marriages, caring for our families, and the myriad responsibilities in life. We try to do it all so well that we neglect ourselves and find ourselves in cruise control —this realization can hit you like a truck or slowly dawn on you. *Born to Buzz* guides you to quit that cruise control and find your passion, taking you on a wonderful journey that explains why it matters, how you'll benefit, and the practical steps to get there. Every woman needs to read this!"

—Loretta Ahmed, founder and CEO of Houbara Communications

"In a world where routine too often dulls our spark, Laura Best dares us to reignite it. Through a compelling blend of storytelling and practical wisdom, she takes readers on a journey to rediscover their passion— not just as a fleeting feeling, but as a force that fuels a life well-lived. She masterfully sets the stage for a powerful exploration of what truly drives us, challenging us to embrace the one life we have, lean into what excites us, and keep our passion alive. With thought-provoking insights and actionable tools, this book is a guide to turning passion into a driving force for life."

—Dr. Tonya Jackman Hampton, author of *The Myth of the Fearless Leader*, speaker, executive coach, and CEO/founder of Sequel Consulting Group

"*Born to Buzz* simply states what we somehow forgot along the way: Passion is LIFE. Through her stories and humorous anecdotes, Laura Best expertly hits you right between the eyes and compels you to prioritize your passions…because you deserve it. I highly recommend this book for anyone wanting to get back to a passion-first life!"

—Teresa Sande, CEO of Mirror Mirror Strategies
and award-winning author of *Find Your Fierce:
Interrupt Imposter Syndrome and Own Your Success*

"Laura Best's inspiring book helps us refocus our purpose on our passions. Her life stories and practical suggestions spark us alive in our work and personal lives. If you are looking out the window of your life wondering if there is something more, it's time for your passions to prevail!"

—Peter H. Bailey, president of The Prouty Project

"Having made a similar journey as Laura Best, I intuitively arrived at the same conclusions. Sadly it took me forty years! *Born to Buzz* is a must-read guide for everything you need to know about believing that you are enough, with lots of Sparks to inspire you on your own journey."

—Val Stones, The *Great British Bake Off*
contestant and author of *The Cake Whisperer*

"*Born to Buzz* speaks to what I value most as a leader: genuine curiosity and passion for making real change happen. I've always believed 'culture is everything,' and Laura Best shows how when we create space for ourselves and our teams to bring their passions to work, we all benefit. Most of all, it reminds us that pursuing what lights us up isn't just for weekends—it belongs at the center of every workplace worth building."

—Jamie Candee, CEO of Edmentum

"Passion invites a full expression of self. Easy enough, right? So why does it feel so hard? Laura Best, with her wit and lived wisdom, provides insights, experiences, and practical ways we can awaken what's already inside of us so we can consistently do the things that light us up."

—Michael Kithcart, CEO of MWK
Consulting and creator of Win Your Way

"Born to Buzz is a beautiful encouragement to allow your life to transcend work, from a friend you didn't know you had. Laura Best writes as if she knows your restlessness personally and shares her philosophy and tangible activities toward awakening your passions. This book is for you if you've ever asked yourself, 'Is this it?'"

—Caitlin Saenz, chief operating officer of
CoverHound Insurance Solutions

"If you're in a slump and need to get your mojo back, set up a coffee date with Laura Best's *Born to Buzz*—a great resource for those who lead with passion and inspire others and are looking to jump-start what's already in your DNA."

—Jayne Haugen Olson, editor in chief of *Mpls. St. Paul Magazine*

"Born to Buzz perfectly explains what so many of us struggle with. Laura Best captures the struggle that forces us to live a life that the world wants us to live, versus the one that truly aligns to our passions. *Born to Buzz* gives us permission to own our passions, even as they evolve."

—Jaime Taets, founder and CEO of
Keystone Group International, author of
The Culture Climb and *You Are Here*, and podcast host
"If you've ever been told to 'follow your passion' but weren't quite sure

what that meant—this book is for you. *Born to Buzz* dives deep into what passion really is, how it's cultivated, and why it's essential for a fulfilling life. This book does a beautiful job of bridging the gap between what excites you and what truly matters. Whether you're searching for clarity or just need a nudge to pursue what lights you up, I highly recommend it."

—Amanda Brinkman, keynote speaker and
creator of The Purpose Pursuit Course

"This is a must-read if you are in your career and want help moving past fear of the unknown and reframing what success means to you. It's time for so many of us to stop crushing ourselves in the process to win and calling it 'ambition.' This book will enable you to have real conversations about passion, identity, and fulfillment at a time when many people don't feel they have permission to support each other or talk openly about their paths to thriving in work and life because it's all connected."

—Olivia Jefferson, social impact executive

"*Born to Buzz* is the rallying cry so many of us didn't know we needed. With humor, heart, and hard-earned wisdom, Laura Best beautifully captures the universal tension between showing up for our responsibilities and showing up for ourselves. Her words remind us that we are allowed—and equipped—to live lives fueled by purpose, joy, and authenticity.

Whether you're standing at a career crossroads or simply feeling the weight of 'fine,' this book is a practical, powerful guide to reigniting your spark without burning everything down. Laura doesn't just offer inspiration—she delivers a road map grounded in relatable stories and bite-sized actions anyone can take."

—Jamie J. Rudolph, chief administrative officer of U.S. Bank.

BORN TO BUZZ

How to Spark Your Passions (Without Quitting It All)

BY LAURA BEST

The concepts and tools presented in the book, especially those discussing trauma, are not meant to be in place of a consultation with a licensed practitioner. The content of this book is for informational purposes only and is not intended to diagnose, treat, cure, or prevent any condition or disease. Please consult with your own mental health specialist regarding the suggestions and recommendations made in this book. The publisher and author make no guarantees concerning the level of success you may experience by following the advice and strategies contained in this book.

This book contains creative nonfiction memoir elements. As such, it is based on my memories as to events and how they occurred. I recognize that characters described in this book may have memories of the events described that are different from my own. Extensive editorial precautions have been taken to ensure diligence to the factual accuracy. Many names and identifying details have been changed to protect their privacy.

Paperback ISBN 13: 978-1-63489-831-7
Printed in the United Kingdom
First Printing: 2026
30 29 28 27 26   5 4 3 2 1

Cover design by Luke Bird
Interior design by Luke Bird and Ngân Huỳnh
Edited by Kristen Tatroe and Sara Letourneau
Proofread by Kerry Stapley and Quinton Singer
Production editing by Lindsay Bohls

Wise Ink Media
PO Box 580195
Minneapolis, MN 55458-0195
WiseInk.com

Wise Ink is a creative publishing agency for game-changers. Wise Ink authors uplift, inspire, and inform, and their titles support building a better and more equitable world. For more information, visit WiseInk.com.

To order, visit ItascaBooks.com or https://www.passioncollective.co/book. Reseller discounts available.

Contact Laura Best at passioncollective.co for speaking engagements and interviews.

This book is dedicated to my dad, Trevor Best.

Dad, you always encouraged me to fly, and you
gave me the energy and belief to do it.

Your hard work, courage, and your passion—for music,
for the Royal Navy, for your friends, and yes, even for
those ejector seat jokes—inspire me to be "me" and
to keep trying to make a difference every day.

This is for you.

TABLE OF CONTENTS

INTRODUCTION   **1**

Nelson Mandela and Me 3
Passion As a Solution 7
How to Use This Book 10
What to Expect 12

PART ONE: GROUNDING   **15**

What Is Passion? 17
Harmonious and Obsessive Passions 21
Why Do We Crave Passion? 36
Living a Passion-First Life 41

PART TWO: SPARKS   **47**

We Deserve It 52
We Know What We Want 58
We Ignore Labels 64
We Refuse to Be Controlled by Comfort 72
We Fuel Ourselves 80
We Find Our People 86
We Transform Our Shame Stories 92

We Craft Our Jobs 98
We Let Go of Certainty 106
We Proudly Dabble 112
We Reach Back to Move Forward 118
We Are Relentlessly Resourceful 124

PART THREE: RISE   **131**

DARE 134

PART FOUR: THE PASSION PROMISE   **147**

ONE LAST WORD   **155**

REFERENCES   **161**

THANK YOU   **169**

ABOUT LAURA BEST   **171**

NOTES   **174**

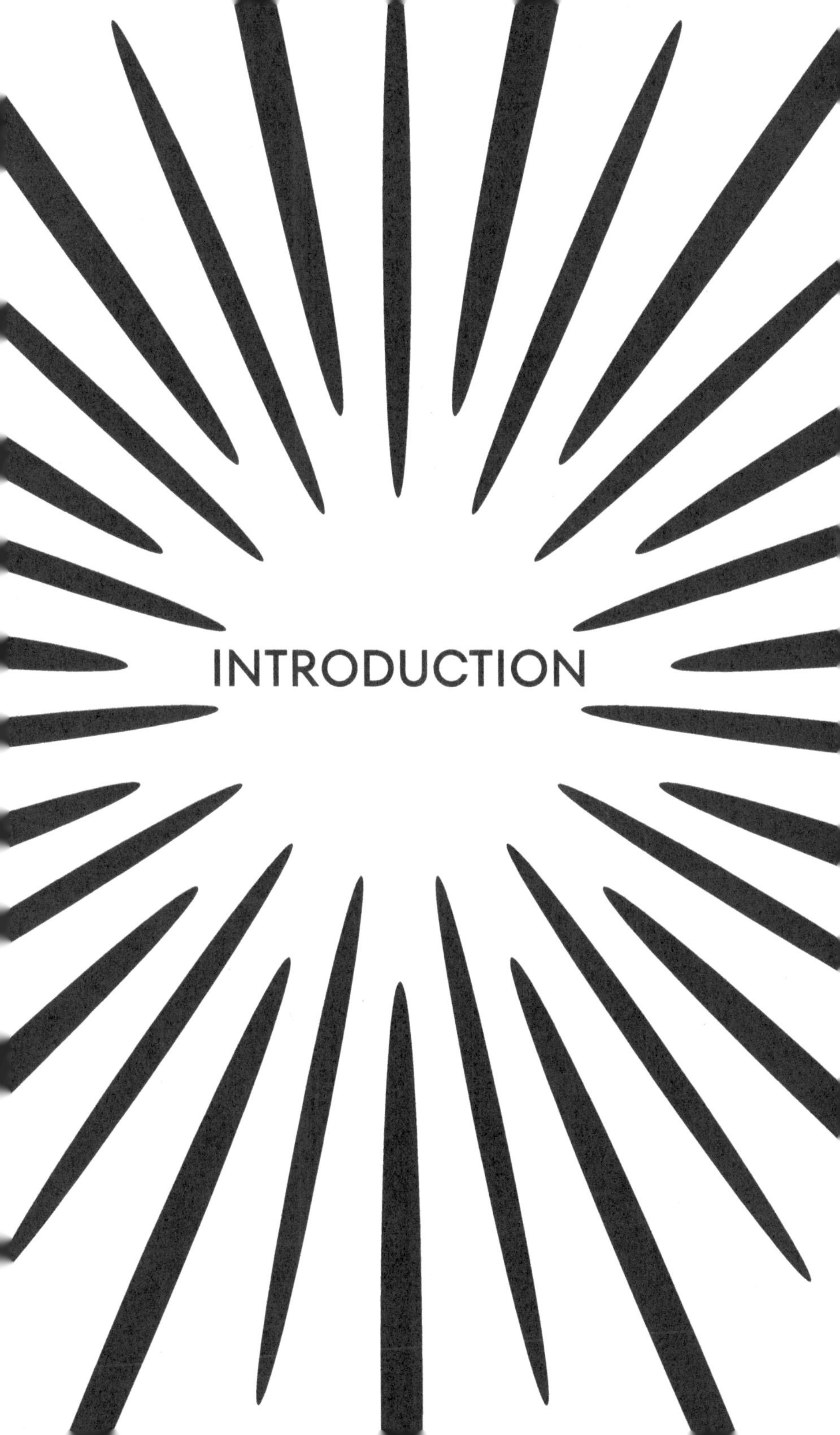

INTRODUCTION

We're smiling, participating, organizing. We're on it, telling ourselves we're "fine." Yet there is a whisper inside of us saying that we could be happier, that we are meant for more, that we are meant to be more.

Nelson Mandela and Me

It was past midnight, and I lay on the dirty departure-gate floor, my laptop case under my head, my coat over my body. I tried to sleep, wondering when I'd get to kiss my daughter, Sophia, good night again. The hard bristles of the filthy carpet dug into my legs as I tried to block out the blaring of the news from the TV monitors telling us that, thousands of miles away, Nelson Mandela had died.

An ice storm had hit Dallas while I was there on a business trip, and now I was stranded at Dallas Fort Worth International Airport. Hotels were full of residents with no power, and the cabs couldn't drive on the ice-stricken roads. Flights had been canceled until further notice, and I was told I'd be lucky to make it home in four days.

This was 2013, and the realization that I was supposed to be leading a successful life was not lost on me. This definitely didn't feel like "success"!

I had one of those high-powered jobs I could only have dreamed of as a young girl in Dorset, England. As one of only a few senior female leaders in a male-dominated, national, technology consulting firm, I was running one team while building a second, leading accounts while pitching new business.

When we won the new client in Dallas, I'd been excited. In addition to the opportunity to do innovative work, the prospect of escaping Minnesota's subzero winter temperatures felt like a gift!

The first few trips had been fun—that familiar honeymoon period with a grateful new client before the complexities revealed themselves. My hotel had felt like a treat, with clean sheets and a breakfast I didn't have to make.

Like many other parents, I felt a responsibility to be at home, keep everything working smoothly, and be there for my family. Yet, a slow, sharp guilt would often take me by surprise. I kept telling myself, "This is what 'successful people' do. They travel. They spend time away from their families. They go to important meetings in offices with clients who need them. This is what men have done for decades, and look! It worked! They're successful, right?"

On the good days, I embraced my status of a full-fledged "road warrior." But after trips six, seven, and eight, I'd begun to feel weary. I was co-leading a multiyear project—was this now my life? I brushed away the doubt and worry, as my jammed schedule wouldn't let me think of the future or my role in it.

On the final day of another trip, I was in my last meeting, with my suitcase by my side, ready to drive to the airport to catch the flight home. As the meeting wrapped up, my boss approached me, seemingly in a mild panic. "Hey, Laura," he said. "We need you to stay for another meeting."

My heart sank. He explained this was a last-minute request, and they needed me to balance out "the other woman," a client who would be attending.

4

You know those situations at work when you're presented with a choice, but it's blatantly obvious that it's not a choice? This was one of those moments. I cared about my work and my team, and I wanted to keep the trust with the team that I'd invested so much in to build. So, I stayed, the meeting was successful (the "woman" ended up being a senior executive), and I was finally free to leave the following day.

Now, if you've ever driven on a Texas highway, you'll know that you need the travel gods on your side. It's truly a feat of concentration and sheer courage with aggressive, multilane driving and roads that seemingly rise into the sky. I was focusing on not dying when my phone rang. It was Brad, the project manager at work.

I'm sure you know, or have worked with, someone like Brad. He's known as a "nice guy"; he's handsome and charismatic, and he knows it. He's "on the track," being positioned for power despite his lack of experience and skills, and he has a manner that implies guaranteed success because he knows he has the system at his back.

"Hey, Laura," said Brad. "I'm checking in because I've noticed you haven't logged enough hours this week."

I kept driving, trying to keep my eyes on the road. Brad made it clear that I needed to be logging more time. I explained that I had maxed my billable hours already, and the week was not yet over. You could say that Brad was simply doing his job, but there was an undercurrent to his request—the invisible power dynamic at play—that gave me a rising feeling of suffocation.

I managed to keep it together despite the traffic raging around me. I ended the call and promptly burst into tears. Huge, gulping, flooding tears.

That was the moment when I realized I had nothing left to give. Nothing.

The only way I can describe it to you is this sense of flatlining inside. I wasn't just tired, I wasn't just burned out—I had lost the spark that made me ME.

It hit me as I drove: Didn't I used to enjoy my work? Didn't I used to get a kick out of it and feel like I was creating something? Didn't I have things I loved to do? What about tennis, baking, reading, and theater? Those things used to be part of who I was, and now I felt miles away from them.

I realized then that I had lost sight of the passion for my work and had let go of the things that lit me up outside of it. I wanted that energy back—the kind that makes life feel rich and full without burning myself (and my family) out in the process. I knew, in that moment, that there had to be a better path ahead.

My journey to create and build Passion Collective had begun.

Passion As a Solution

Back then, even though on the outside all looked good, I felt that there was something missing. Shouldn't I be grateful, lucky to be independent and loved, a Brit living the American Dream?

I was grateful. That wasn't the problem, and no amount of gratitude journaling was going to help me.

Years later, after meeting thousands of "Passion Seekers" and having done the research for this book, I now see that I was experiencing a universal challenge.

This is the challenge of loving our lives despite its obligations, responsibilities, and hardships. We're smiling, participating, organizing. We're on it, telling ourselves we're "fine." Yet there is a whisper inside of us saying that we could be happier, that we are meant for more, that we are meant to be more.

We daren't admit it, because it feels like a self-indulgent betrayal to our families and those who are part of that life.

We daren't admit it, because who are we to focus on joy when the world is in turmoil?

We daren't admit it, because we have invested too much time and money into our careers, identities, and lives to question it.

We daren't admit it, because we don't have an answer to what would make us love life more, and that makes us feel empty inside.

We daren't admit it, because we believe that our privilege stops us from wanting more.

We daren't admit it, because we think we're the only one who feels this way.

Yet, this craving for more—this desire for connection, enjoyment, energy, and meaning—is not happening in a vacuum:

* We have never been more disengaged from our work. Over 50 percent of workers in large UK-based organizations are disengaged from their work, causing pain for people and impacting business for organizations.

* The gender pay gap refuses to close. At best, women are getting paid three-quarters of the salaries of men. Essentially, that's working three months of the year for free. (Let that sink in...)

* Unhappiness is growing for many. From 2006 to 2010, the happiness of young people has dramatically declined compared to later generations, and women report being unhappier now than in 1996.

* The world is in turmoil. At least seventeen wars have been started since 2000, many of which are still being fought today.

It is hardly surprising that we are craving the need to rediscover the things that light us up and give us satisfaction, joy, a sense of accomplishment, togetherness, and contribution.

The challenge comes in the how. How, in our back-to-back scheduled days, do we create the space, resources, and energy to do "more"? Isn't doing more of what we love a dream—or, at best, a nice-to-have wish?

I believe it is the opposite of a dream, that it should be a reality for us all. In fact, I believe it is our obligation to discover and pursue the things we love in work and in life.

We have been given—by whatever higher power or science you believe in—a unique spirit, a set of talents and magic that, when combined, can create the most beautiful moments, feelings, and contributions to this world.

To push those down—to ignore them, to purposefully not invest in them—is a tragedy.

We have one life to live here on Earth. Just one. And yet, we're waiting for the perfect moment, the next vacation, the retirement that is fifteen years away, or the bucket list to actually spend time doing things that help us feel and do good.

What if we can live a life where we put our passions first? What would that look like? How might that positively affect us and those we love?

This is the reason for this book.

How to Use This Book

In September 2023, I left the stage at the biggest speaking engagement of my career so far. Until then, I had mostly stood behind the Passion Collective community, where I felt satisfaction in helping them inspire and support each other.

In the audience, I saw hundreds of people from all backgrounds, genders, job titles, and locations reconnecting with the things they loved and sharing that energy with others. The universality of "pursuing your passion" was right there in front of me.

A few days later, an attendee emailed to say my keynote had inspired her to ask for a long overdue promotion—and she got it! I was blown away! Who knew what domino effect this one event had created—and may be continuing to create? At that moment, I knew I had to gather my beliefs, experiences, and knowledge into a book that could help people rediscover their passions in work and life. I had to keep those dominoes falling.

I built Passion Collective on a philosophy of "Practical Inspiration." We need inspiration to activate our motivation and belief, but that inspiration only matters when we can apply it to our real lives. That can be incredibly difficult to plan for, because each chapter of our journey brings different demands on our time and energy.

Sometimes we're flying high, and other times, out of nowhere, our world can turn black with loss, trauma, or grief, and we have no choice but to simply make it through.

After my miscarriage, the last thing I needed to hear in those months of raw grief was "do more of what lights you up." And, when my beloved father died while I tried to navigate a challenging job, my world spun so fast that I couldn't even tell you what I thought or desired for months.

Life may also hand you an ongoing sadness or challenge—perhaps a layoff, divorce, or medical treatment—that creates a fog of inertia and worry that is hard to escape.

That's why, regardless of which chapter of life you're experiencing, I know that your time and energy are both precious and unpredictable. I've written this book for you to get lost in over a rainy weekend, or to dip into whenever you need guidance or inspiration. No judgment: "you do you," as they say!

What to Expect

Part one will explain what passion is. It's a complex topic, with thousands of years' worth of philosophers and academics defining it in different ways. I'll introduce you to a model that will change how you think about passion and how it can help you. Consider this your warm-up!

In part two, I'll give you the how. I've written twelve "Sparks"—each one a commitment that we, as Passion Seekers, make to ourselves about bringing more passion into our lives. Think of these Sparks as promises about how to show up in the world, even on our busiest or most challenging days. Each one comes with a Passion Prompt that will give you space to reflect, journal, and plan. Read them all at once, or one at a time with your morning coffee. Do whatever is most helpful to you.

It's one thing to spark our passions, and another to keep the "buzz" alive in real life. Part three gives you practical ways to define and move forward with your passions, pick yourself up when you stumble, and nurture what matters most—even when it feels out of reach.

And finally, part four will give you a way to take your next step, which is so crucial in making change happen in your life. Don't skip this part!

I hope that you hold this book close to your heart—that it gives you renewed belief in your talents and strength and a fierce determination to pursue the passions that help you truly live *your* life.

Let's get started!

PART ONE:
GROUNDING

When we engage with our true passions—or even when we're just beginning to transform an interest into a great love—we generate an energy, a "buzz", that creates immediate, long-term benefits for ourselves and those around us.

What Is Passion?

The study of passion over the centuries by philosophers and academics has been the study of humanity—of our souls, emotions, and why we do what we do and love what we love. Passion can be pleasure; it can be pain. Passions can bring on the downfall of civilization, or according to the philosopher Hegel, "nothing great in this world has ever been accomplished without passion."

Depending on your source, passions can be fed but can't be found; they are fleeting, or they are forever; they are true, or they are an error in judgment; they can be avoided, or they can be tamed; they are chains, or they are freedom; they can drive us to good or evil.

Confused yet?!

Things get even foggier when we look at passion's cultural baggage, which has become embedded in our languages and cultures. Here are just three examples:

"Slave to Passion": This phrase took on a life of its own after originating from Scottish philosopher David Hume, who said, "Reason is, and ought only to be, the slave of the passions and can never pretend to any other office than to serve and obey them." Passion feels like a negative, something we want to avoid or would feel ashamed of, because it implies an abandonment of sense. (Read Hume's quote closely, however, and you'll realize that he actually said that passion and reason work together—that passions lead us in life, and reason supports this.)

"The Passion of Christ": This is the story of Jesus's final days, from his arrest to his crucifixion. For Christians, this phrase refers to an intensely painful belief full of agony, betrayal, and suffering.

"Crime of Passion": These crimes are typically committed in the "heat of the moment," driven by anger, revenge, jealousy, or lust. In historical cases, they were treated more leniently; and in many instances, this term was used to defend violent crimes against women.

From these three definitions, you'd be forgiven for assuming that passion is not exactly something to aspire to! Who needs that association with darkness, shame, and complication?

I became confused—why was I drawn to this word, this concept, when clearly it was so divisive and unclear? I set out to find a definition that would guide me and the community I wanted to build.

My first assumption was that passion is an emotion, but I was swiftly proven wrong.

In 2017, Alan S. Cowen and Dacher Keltner, both PhDs, expanded on a 1977 theory about the number of emotions that exist. Instead of the commonly assumed twelve, they claimed that there are twenty-seven:

* admiration
* adoration
* aesthetic appreciation
* amusement
* anxiety
* awe
* awkwardness
* boredom
* calmness
* confusion
* craving
* disgust
* empathic pain
* entrancement
* envy
* excitement
* fear
* horror
* interest
* joy
* nostalgia
* romance
* sadness
* satisfaction
* sexual desire
* sympathy
* triumph

Note that passion isn't on that list, even though emotions are defined as (wait for it) "conscious mental reactions subjectively experienced as strong feelings usually directed toward a specific object and typically accompanied by physiological and behavioral changes in the body."

I'm no psychologist, but to me, passion can feel like an emotion, *and* a feeling (how we interpret our emotions). Things get even more confusing when you realize that "passion" can also describe an activity (horse-riding is my passion!).

So, on the one hand, passion is an ethereal, invisible reaction; on the other, it's a clearly defined activity. As I dug deeper, I found myself getting sent in circles.

Then, I found the work of Robert J. Vallerand and his colleagues, who claim that passion is a *motivational* force, something that inspires us to act. They tell us that a passion is a "strong inclination toward a specific object, activity, concept, or person that we 'love' or strongly like."

Yes! Now it became clear—passion was an energy inside of us, a life force that is truly ours. Only we know how passion feels and how it motivates or sustains us. This also means that passion is a way of moving through the world, a style of showing up, of bringing that motivational force into rooms, teams, or communities; of sharing our strengths, beliefs, and ideas with the world.

As I dug deeper, I learned that Vallerand and his colleagues defined a passion as something we:

* Highly value (i.e., the objective, activity, concept, or person must be meaningful to us)

* Consistently invest time and energy into (i.e., a passion isn't something we typically try once or twice)

* Consider part of our identity (e.g., we are comfortable including our passion when we describe ourselves to others)

This seems reasonable, even clear, about what a passion is and how we can identify it. Passion *can* be found. It *can* be generated, it *can* be shared, and it *can* be experienced. Passion doesn't just need to be work-related. The key is thinking about how all of these notions connect to make us happier and more fulfilled.

Harmonious and Obsessive Passions

Vallerand and his colleagues didn't just stop with their helpful definition. They continued to share that there are, in fact, two distinct types of passion: harmonious and obsessive.

Harmonious Passion

As you might expect from its name, *harmonious passion* complements our lives and those around us. It fuels us. It gives us energy, peace, and calm. It makes us smile, drives us forward. It can become part of our identity in a good way. You may have experienced this if you've asked someone at a networking event what they "do" and they responded: "I'm Susan, I'm a corporate HR exec, and I also love rock climbing!"

Interestingly, Vallerand and his colleagues also found that harmonious passions often satisfy three of our fundamental human needs.

Harmonious Passions Give Us Autonomy

We humans tend to be happier when we feel we have some control

over our tasks and our path ahead. However, as we build our lives, often chasing success, we find that we have to sacrifice our autonomy.

While companies often claim that they offer autonomy to their people, the reality rarely matches the intention. More often than not, bureaucracy, inefficient collaboration practices, and corporate politics stifle the promise of autonomy that attracts employees in the first place.

If you think I sound cynical, you may be right—for good reason!! Believe it or not, there is a syndrome called NAG (you couldn't ask for a better acronym), which stands for "No Authority Gauntlet." It is based on the idea of accountability without authority. I have held many NAG positions in my career. I've been asked to lead projects that were purportedly "mission critical" but lacked budget or skilled team members. I've been directed to merge departments when senior leadership had no desire to make changes to realize that transformation. In one particularly challenging job environment, my manager, who was trying to force growth, asked me to befriend (and report back on) coworkers.

In our personal lives, autonomy can fade gradually as our commitments grow. We find partners and build shared lives, raise families, and take on caregiving responsibilities for aging parents or other loved ones. Each step may bring joy and meaning but can also quietly diminish our ability to choose and act independently.

We try to reclaim our autonomy in small ways. We make self-care lists of "me time." We shut the door to watch the Netflix show that we want for an hour. We tell ourselves that the remodeling project can have our stamp on it, or the family vacation can be our decision

on where to go and what to do. Yet we wonder: do we have any real autonomy when so many people depend on us?

This is why harmonious passion is so important, because it gives us opportunities for autonomy, even if it's only for a sliver of time in our week.

Over the years, I've seen Passion Seekers prove this in various ways:

* Volunteering for a work committee which gives the opportunity to use their creativity to create something that others will benefit from.

* Rediscovering an individual sport and loving how reliant they are on their own skills and decisions in a game.

* Learning how to knit, because despite the pattern to follow, they can decide the colors, the yarn, the when and where of how to knit, and for whom the knitting is done.

* Writing their first novel, because when they write, they're the only one who can map out the characters' paths.

Autonomy is precious—these moments, however small, let us reclaim a piece of ourselves.

Harmonious Passions Give Us Competency

The second basic human need that harmonious passions satisfy is that of competence.

Striving for competence is a double-edged sword. We all know that to succeed—especially at work—we need to perform, to go "above

and beyond" to get the job done. Forward motion is no longer about meeting expectations. And, investing time and energy into skill building can be truly satisfying.

However, the demand of "competence" can begin to feel like we are leaving little room for our passions to shine. If we're solely striving for performance without a connection to what lights us up inside, the effort of creating and sustaining high-performing careers can take precedence over our happiness and fulfilment.

This isn't because we lack the desire to learn or improve. Typically, the reason is that to become adept (to "get good") at what we do, to keep up with our annual performance reviews and build our reputations, we have no choice but to learn on the job, often by trial and error and a lack of professional instruction. It can resemble mental gymnastics and political game-playing rather than the learning that we crave, the learning that gives us a sense of personal accomplishment.

If you are a woman, a person of color, or a member of any other underrepresented group, you also have little choice but to navigate systematic bias and discrimination which demands invisible standards or competence that others are not asking to comply with. Which is why, when academics say that harmonious passions fulfill a need for competence, we need to be thoughtful about how to apply the term.

While we think we should feed a desire for competence, what we actually crave is a guarantee against failure. Out of all the barriers that cause Passion Seekers to hesitate or stop pursuing their passions, a fear of "sucking"—of missing the mark, hurting ourselves, or looking silly—is always the greatest.

24

Instead, I prefer to think of competence this way: A desire or curiosity to improve is a hallmark of a harmonious passion. It's the feeling you get when you try something new, and you realize you're not as good at it as you expected (because you're used to a feeling of competency in your job). You accept that you have a long way to go, perhaps with a rueful smile . . . and you feel a kernel of curiosity inside about how to do just a little bit better next time.

This acknowledgement, this desire to grow, contributes to our feeling of well-being because it's us believing in ourselves again. It's letting go, just a wee bit, of our perfectionist tendencies to give ourselves the opportunity to fail so we can introduce something new— something nourishing or fulfilling—into our lives. The willingness to fail is self-respect. It's us acknowledging that we deserve to add to our experience and fulfillment in some way.

I know how this feels. One Minnesota winter, after weeks of subzero temperatures, thick black ice, and dark, short days, my cabin fever had set in with a vengeance. (I never feel more British than during a Minnesotan winter, where I crave rain over snow and the ability to stride down a muddy country lane with greenery still around me and a warm pub at the end.) When you're in the depths of winters like this, the feeling is similar to a lockdown. A sort of suffocation, and an achy boredom, can pervade everything you do.

I knew I needed to get out, to create. On a whim, I signed up for a community-education pottery class. My inspiration, I kid you not, was the film *Ghost* (remember Patrick Swayze and Demi Moore? Who can forget?!) and I thought, *Well, that looks like fun! How hard can it be?* I was right . . . and wrong. The fun was the messiness and the feeling of being an absolute beginner in a room of specialist equipment and people who seemed to know what they were doing.

That didn't intimidate me, though. It energized me, giving me a break from being the one who was always expected to have answers, instead giving me the role of question asker, of explorer.

As I spun that pottery wheel, squelching my fingers into the clay, splashing water everywhere, I realized I was having pure FUN. I was experiencing the liberation of not worrying about the mess, of simply giving something a go. Instead of worrying that my performance was being judged, I laughed at the fact that I didn't have a clue what I was doing. As I felt the coolness of the clay, its movement underneath my hands, I realized I was doing something—albeit badly—that others had mastered. It was a feeling of embarking on a journey without a map, trusting the guides around me.

After the initial exhilaration came the hard part. While I knew that pottery was an art, little did I know how touch, nuance, and skill were essential in making a thumb pot. (Something that, by the way, my toddler daughter had brought home from daycare and had seemingly mastered.) My clay wobbled only seconds after I'd plunged my thumbs in to shape it, with me desperately trying to stop it from flying off into the instructor's face. I tried again, and again, and again. At one point, I cried tears of frustration, desperately trying to wipe them away with my muddy hands before the others saw me. Demi Moore had made it look so easy! I had thought I'd be "good" at this. I had thought it would be easy, like how it looks on YouTube! I had thought I'd feel "at one" with the clay!

Oh no, my body and soul told me during class. *That is not the point.* I had a feeling of not wanting this to beat me and wanting to be good at it. I began asking more questions during my classes and Googling YouTubers like Ingleton Pottery, who sent me down rabbit holes of fascination. It was there that I watched how you're meant to caress

and manipulate the clay. How the experts were covered in mess, often in their equally chaotic workshops. How much clay, concentration, and skill they used to get to something that looked perfect.

When my community-ed classes came to an end, I knew that it was something I felt a connection with. However, I didn't pursue it.

I'll get a pottery wheel at the house! I thought. Then a voice in my head, which I'll call "Passion Killer," nipped that in the bud by saying, *Where on earth would you put it? It would make such a mess!*

"I'll do it on Sundays!" I responded.

But Passion Killer said, *But you'll never have the time. Remember the household stuff you need to catch up with?*

"Then I'll sign up for another class!" I told myself.

Passion Killer replied, *Who would you go with? You wouldn't want to do it alone this time, would you?*

"But I'd enjoy learning it!" I said.

Passion Killer said, *How would you know where to start?*

I didn't pursue pottery in the end. The potential was there—all the elements of a harmonious passion waiting to bloom. But "Passion Killer" succeeded in showing me the gulf between where I was and where I wanted to be, rubbing my beginner's awkwardness in my face. I saw the mountain of practice ahead, the countless misshapen bowls and irregular edges I'd have to create before achieving anything close to mastery, and I let that voice win.

Yet, pottery hasn't given up on me, even if I temporarily gave up on it. It finds ways to catch my attention—through Instagram reels of perfectly centered clay, through conversations at parties with people who light up describing their latest glazing experiments. "Really?" I'll say. "Where do you do it? How did you start?" And while I haven't taken that next step yet, the fact that these questions still spark something inside tells me something important. The fact that I still want to learn, that I'm still drawn to understand this craft, suggests that pottery still may have a chapter in my story. The curiosity I have for gaining competence in it feels like a comfort against the daily grind, like a piece of cake you save until later. For now, I've simply set it aside—a potential harmonious passion waiting for the right moment, perhaps during one of Minnesota's long winters, when I'm ready to embrace being a beginner again.

Harmonious Passions Help Us Feel Connected

We have never been more connected, and yet never more lonely.

The final basic human need that Vallerand and his colleagues say is a sign of a true harmonious passion is *relatedness*, the idea that when we're more connected with others and ourselves, we are happier and more fulfilled.

The word *relatedness* feels distant. (Maybe it's the word's similarity to *relative*, a person in your family who isn't as close to you as others?) I prefer to think about it as a type of connection, which can show up as a connection to others, to a cause, or to ourselves.

Connecting to Others

The pace and distraction of modern life make true connection a tough business. A study commissioned by Fisherman's Friend

claims that we need to invest thirty-four hours to move from a superficial acquaintance to friendship! Add to that the popularity of virtual tools, 24/7 demand, and robot customer service, and it's no wonder that we feel a growing sense of disconnection from others.

A harmonious passion will give you opportunities to renew and create connections, regardless of how small the interaction may be. Your new class at the gym may give you an hour of laughter and shared effort. The art that you posted on social media may inspire a comment from someone who tells you it lifted their spirits. The mentoring project you led at work may result in new career paths for the people you helped.

Connection with others doesn't just mean friendship. Rather, a harmonious passion can help you see the value of connections of all types.

Connecting to a Cause

With the twenty-four-hour news cycle, we are never too far away from a tragedy, an issue, or a situation that needs help. However, despite the demand for support, it has never felt more difficult to contribute in a way that connects our talents and uniqueness to the cause.

I've spoken to many Passionados who felt burned out from volunteering. Why? Because they were following the "shoulds." They were doing the food-packing because their church had set it up. They were the Girl Scout leaders, since no other parents would volunteer. They told me time and again, "Laura, I want to give back, but it bores me. Then I feel guilty, so I don't do it—and then I feel even more guilty!"

When we do what we think we *should* do, the result is that we spend our time doing things that *don't* fill us up out of obligation, or we avoid them because we know they won't give us what we seek. Or we feel guilty for using the opportunity as a source for our own fulfillment.

When your unique talents naturally flow into a cause you care about—and it energizes your life while helping others—that's harmonious passion at its best.

Connection to Ourselves

Connection to ourselves can be elusive during a hectic week. For some, that looks like quiet time each morning or evening to reconnect with our intentions, emotions, and energy. For others, it can mean clocking off the shift and throwing ourselves into a creative pursuit that gives a sense of escape.

A harmonious passion inspires and nurtures this connection, and helps us remember and reclaim who we are, inside and out. You may hear a Passion Seeker say that one of their passions helps them "feel like myself" or get a better sense of what they believe and why.

Connection to the self doesn't just mean meditation or yoga. One of my passions is genealogy—I've spent countless hours down the rabbit hole of Ancestry.com to create my family tree. I'm not a precise genealogist (I'm too impatient), but where my competency and *curiosity* lie are in making connections between random things—names, places, and people—and having the persistence and motivation to follow through. I found the name of one of my great-grandfathers this way, matching a photo to records and a hastily spoken history from my aunt. The feeling of connection to this man, and ultimately to myself, was unforgettable.

Obsessive Passion

Find what you love and let it kill you. Let it drain you of your all. Let it cling onto your back and weigh you down into eventual nothingness. Let it kill you and let it devour your remains.

—Supposedly attributed to a letter
written by Charles Bukowski

An *obsessive passion* is as you would expect—exactly the opposite of a harmonious passion. It is an activity that you feel compelled to undertake that can harm or destroy you, your relationships, and the things you hold dear in life. Pretty scary, right?!

Pressure often drives obsessive passions. This can look like pressure for social acceptance, self-esteem, or uncontrolled excitement. It's a feeling that means you simply cannot help but engage. This type of passion is impulsive, manipulative, and sometimes dangerous, and it is where addictions burrow away at our souls and happiness.

Obsessive passions are sneaky. They can show up as harmonious passions and seem like worthy endeavors. Many people you follow on social media are likely pursuing obsessive passions but have learned how to present them in a way that seems the opposite so they can gather the acceptance, kudos, and self-respect they crave.

Think of workaholism. Have you ever been that person who, when asked during an interview, "What's the worst habit you have at work?" answered the way we were all trained to in the '80s, '90s, or early 2000s, "Well, if you were to push me, I'd say that I can sometimes just get too dedicated to my work," or "Sometimes people tell me that I am just so persistent with details and getting things done." Come on, we've all done it!

This response was intended to show us as the servant employee, the good soldier who would jump off the cliff for the boss's or company's vision. We're just so passionate about getting the job done, we work SO damn hard, and you should hire us!

In real life, people who don't see beyond the true purpose of this claim have different troubles. Their passion for work gets dark. It begins to take over their home life, with sneaked-in emails at the dinner table, 7:00 a.m. Zoom calls, weekend work "to get ahead," and an obsession with moving up or over others. The drive to succeed becomes a drive to win at all costs—or, for some, to simply keep up with a fire hose of work and expectations that can rarely be fully met. Work becomes a "passion" that defines everything in someone's life to the point of neglecting health, family, and happiness.

Obsessive passions are not easy to understand or explain. It is easy to judge those who do put themselves into situations we cannot imagine or, frankly, wouldn't even dream of.

A terrible example of this is the passion project that turned into tragedy with the implosion of the *Titan* submarine in 2023. Did you notice how the media talked about the "passion" of Stockton Rush, the CEO of OceanGate, who was described after his death as "the last of the American dreamers"? Or how Shahzada Dawood and his son, Suleman, were described as having "cherished a shared passion for adventure and exploration of all the world had to offer them"?

Passion, in these cases, is referenced not as an excuse per se, but as a way of reasoning as to why people would invest their precious lives—and the lives of others around them—when, to regular humans, the risk is so great.

It's not that people with obsessive passions are following them blindly. They're doing so knowing and accepting the immediate risk. As Hamish Harding, another passenger on the *Titan*, once said about his passion for exploration, "My view is that these are all calculated risks and are well understood before we start."

What stokes this desire to "be the first," or to do something bigger, bolder, and more extreme than others? Ironically, the drivers are the same as those for harmonious passions:

* The *relatedness* with the team.

* The *connection* with the history of the *Titanic* and those who lost their lives. (Stockton Rush's wife, Wendy, is the great-great-granddaughter of Isidor and Ida Straus, who died in the *Titanic* wreck after letting women and children escape before them.)

* The *competency* of being the first ones to solve a puzzle, operate machinery, understand technical details, or have the mental strength to forgo the dangers of the adventure. (Imagine the dinner party conversation that would have followed if they'd survived: "Weren't you scared? What training did you do? How many years have you spent learning about the *Titanic*?")

* The *autonomy* of being five passengers, alone in a vast ocean, navigating their own submarine to depths that only a few people have seen.

These are, after all, basic human needs, so it shouldn't surprise us that they are sourced in both types of passions. The challenge is how, as humans, we serve those needs.

We try to understand how these individuals could risk everything in ways that may seem like folly, or rich people's games. However, that would dismiss the deep pull that obsessive passions can have. These passions are not just knitting in the evenings, taking on extra work projects, or signing up for 10k charity races. People who pursue obsessive passions feel that if they don't, a part of them doesn't get to live. Often, it can literally be what they "live for" at the end of a long week, or a balance to a job they may be slogging through out of duty for family or societal expectations.

For those who love or support a person with an obsessive passion, the line is equally hard to navigate. We see how this activity fires up, sustains, and drives this person; and we may love the energy that we see. Often, we admire the person and marvel at their courage, commitment, or even their daredevilry. We may be fiercely proud of their accomplishments despite the danger to themselves or others. We don't realize this activity is an obsessive passion until that person, or others like them, begin to get hurt. Sometimes, these wounds are small, easily covered with a literal or theoretical Band-Aid. Other times, this damage can be physical to them, to property, or to financial or relationship stability.

And yet, even if those we love persist with the activity that is beginning to risk damage—literally "daring the devil"—we still support them. We never want to be the person who tells them to dial things back. Who wants to be a killjoy when clearly this person is loving life so much when they're pursuing this activity? But there is also a deeper part of us that is scared of what will happen if our loved one stops this activity, which often isn't as tangibly dangerous as jumping off cliffs. Will they lose their "lust for life"? Will they stop being as fun and engaged? Would this signal the beginning of a middle-aged decline from which there is no return?

Take, for example, Lee Meyer from Nebraska, who was so enamored with gigantic, horned Watusi bulls that he procured one, named it "Howdy Doody," then proceeded to drive down the freeway with the bull riding shotgun in his car. (If this sounds reasonable to you, then do take a look at the video of Lee proudly showing off Howdy Doody—and his customized car—to the police officer!)

I'm sure Lee would tell you that he is passionate about this breed of bull for all sorts of reasons. To him, it seems perfectly normal to ride with his BFF next to him (where were they going, do you think?!). But to other humans, every risk imaginable comes to mind. (Getting speared by a horn! Disease! Rampage!)

That's the thing about obsessive passions: We can't understand or rationalize them. What we can do, though, is understand the difference between them and the type of passion we want to create or pursue. (Hint: It's not the obsessive type.) It's to balance our desire to feel *alive* and our enthusiasm to pursue new things that light us up, with respect for the lives we have been given and for those who love us. It's acknowledging and getting help when we feel ourselves slipping into the obsessive passion zone—when it's starting to take over our lives or impact others negatively—instead of persisting.

Why Do We Crave Passion?

The call to passion isn't always convenient—it certainly wasn't for me as a new parent in a demanding job. I do still, sometimes, have my days when I wonder why it was that I couldn't just stay "on track," whether that would have somehow been easier than the path I have taken.

Desire for more passion in our work or life rarely follows the rules we have obeyed as we've built our careers or lives. It shows up as scattered jigsaw pieces—a forgotten hobby that pops back into our memory, a fascination with other people's creative pursuits, envy about a friend's accomplishment, or a nagging feeling that there's something waiting to be expressed. These cravings might seem random or even silly against the backdrop of our busy lives, yet they can persist, like taps on the shoulder from our deeper selves.

We Want to Express Our Creativity

Remember Jennifer Aniston's character in the film *Office Space* and how she eventually plucked up the courage to quit over the amount of "flair" she was being required to wear in her job as a server? She had fifteen pieces of "flair" on her uniform, but her supervisor was "suggesting" she wear thirty-seven. The "flair" were little buttons,

all made by the restaurant chain, that were awarded to employees for various expressions of corporate-approved behavior (mostly showing passion for their work).

This forced display of enthusiasm is just one example of how work can box us in. (I still cringe at the memory of the "Mandatory Fun" that one company I worked for insisted upon. And yes, that was its official name . . .) You may be lucky enough to work in a role that enables you to express yourself without getting fired—and better yet, you've joined an organization that fosters creativity. But many people, once they've clocked in the hours of their job and returned home for the "second shift" of parenting or caring for others, have little energy or motivation to express what's inside of them. Worse, on our bad days, we forget why creativity is so important. It begins to feel like work. It becomes much easier to simply comply, to get through the weeks, building our lives in the best way we can. Creativity can feel like a luxury, or an inconvenience.

We Miss Laughter

Laughter demands that we show up as ourselves. We need to feel safe, unjudged, and connected with others, regardless of whatever silly, hilarious, or ridiculous thing sets off our giggles to break our professional molds, even if just for a minute.

Sometimes, an absence of that type of laughter can be a sign that we are disconnected from ourselves and others in an entirely different way.

When I was a corporate marketing leader, I hired a group of my former advertising colleagues to help our organization with a brand project. We'd worked together previously, they understood my dry English sense of humor, and I understood their Minnesotan style (I think!). At one point, we began brainstorming, and I can't remember what set us off, but it wasn't long before we had tears streaming down our faces. You know, the type where you snort, and you begin talking, and you can't finish the sentence because your body just wants to LAUGH? Oh, it was fun!

What I remember most is the feeling that I hadn't laughed at work for a long, long time. I remember the pang of sadness when I realized that. And then, I noticed how I craved more of it.

For me, it was another data point about the path I was creating. I knew I needed to find (or create) space where lightness and laughter could coexist with truly caring about my work. Now, if you come and see one of my keynotes, you'll notice that I'm almost like a stand-up comedian in parts. That's intentional; the power of laughter, release, and connection is something I craved, and so now I create it for myself and others.

We Have "Unanswered Callings"

In 1985, sociologist Robert N. Bellah and his colleagues defined three different ways that Americans viewed their work. Some see work as a job, a means to an end, and a way to pay the bills while still having time for a nonwork life. For others, work is a career to be built, invested in, sacrificed for, and a means of accomplishment and status. And finally, a minority see their work as a "calling" and find great fulfillment and enjoyment from the contribution they are making to society.

Work can just be work; and for many happy people, it's exactly

that. Others love their careers and create pride and legacy from them. Callings are another matter and often get confused with the concept of passion.

An increasing number of people are realizing they have an "unanswered calling," an occupation (or part of an occupation) that feels like part of who they are. They are drawn to it repeatedly, yet they are not pursuing it. That can come in the form of hitting a big milestone at work, then looking back over your career and asking yourself, "How did I get *here*?" Or it can come as a realization that the field you've entered with all good intentions of making a difference is giving you limited or no opportunity to do so in the way that you want.

It can hurt to ignore an unanswered calling. I've seen people simply shrug in sad resignation that their calling was in a "former life," and I've seen others experience negative reactions of resentment—or worse. If we leave these unanswered callings alone for too long, sometimes we can feel intimidated about exploring them. The promise of the impact we might be able to make fights with the knowledge that we might need to practice, retrain, or put ourselves out there again. The calling doesn't matter, we say. The job comes first. And that may simply be the chapter of life you find yourself in.

Our passions give us a way to generate the fulfillment that our "calling" may have provided, without the risk of abstaining from our duties to our family or team. For example, even if we can't quit our job as a mechanical engineer to be a soccer coach or give up the finance CEO career to become a songwriter, it doesn't mean that we can't make a difference to others, that we can't enjoy an activity. Our "calling" can be what we make it. However, even with this belief, finding a way to rediscover, find, nurture, pursue, and sustain our

passions is not easy. In some cases, we see our passions as a list of activities that we need to weave into our busy lives (which is where they so often fall to the bottom of the list). In others, the thought of redesigning our lives to fit in our passions feels impossible and often like a selfish endeavor.

Living a Passion-First Life

Here is where living a Passion-First Life comes in.

What if you began to put your passions *first* in life, without dismissing or denigrating the people, activities, and commitments that you want to honor? This isn't about upending your entire life—it's about discovering what truly lights you up and finding practical, realistic ways to pursue those things so that you and those you care for can be happier.

"My life is fine," some tell me when we talk about paths in life. "I'm paying my mortgage. I do things I like. My family is healthy. I have a job." And they're right—life can be perfectly adequate without actively pursuing our passions.

But here's the truth: "Fine" can quietly steal our strength, our magic, and all that is unique in us.

Forgive me if I'm presenting this in a way that seems like an easy choice. Far from it—in today's world, we're presented with two seemingly opposite sides. On one hand, there's "hustle culture"—the relentless pressure to always be "on," always performing, always succeeding. Scroll through social media on any Monday morning, and you might think this mindset has taken over the world.

On the other, there's the pushback, beautifully captured in a viral blog titled "What If All I Want Is a Mediocre Life?" written by Krista O'Reilly-Davi-Digui, who had lost a child to suicide and faced numerous health challenges. The piece resonated with countless people who felt broken or wrong for not fitting into our achievement-obsessed culture. "Am I simply not enough?" she asks, for wanting to live life on her own terms.

A Passion-First Life offers a different path altogether. It recognizes that passion isn't one-size-fits-all. For some, passion means striving for excellence, winning awards, or building a successful business. For others, it can be a private creative activity, never to see the light of day. What matters is that the passion is yours, and that it is fuel for the stage of life you find yourself in.

When we engage with our true passions—or even when we're just beginning to transform an interest into a great love—we generate an energy, a "buzz," that creates immediate, long-term benefits for ourselves and those around us. We're not just doing what we love; we're honoring, nurturing, and sharing our unique magic with the world. This energy shouldn't be an optional extra—it's essential to living the lives we were given. Our lives are ours to make of them, including the tragedies, joys, challenges, and love. When we merely accept that everything is "fine" for fear of rocking the boat or because we don't believe we deserve more, we rob ourselves and others of the opportunity to feel more alive and to make contributions, no matter how small, to the goodness in life. What's more, it's been scientifically proven that pursuing harmonious passions helps with our self-esteem, our ability to connect to others, and our concentration, mindfulness, and physical and mental health.

One way I help Passion Seekers realize and remember these benefits is by remembering "LIFE":

42

L (Love)

When we are actively pursuing the things we love, a wonderful thing starts happening inside us. We begin to love ourselves more. We begin to appreciate our quirks, our talents, and the things our bodies and brains do so easily that make us special. We simply start feeling something again after years of numbing ourselves or ignoring our emotions, needs, and desires.

When this happens, we soften our edges with those we love. We create space in our hearts and our days to give the extra hug or kiss, send the extra thank-you note, or take a breath when our child has taken the last phone charger (again). We more confidently set and uphold our boundaries with others. We feel more able to take our "place at the "table" at work, or to reach out to those who may benefit from our support.

When we remember what "love" looks and feels like, it becomes far easier to identify others who could be part of a tribe that can help and support us. And when we know more about what we love, it becomes far easier to turn away from what will harm us or others.

I (Imagination)

Do you miss your imagination? I certainly did back in 2014. As a child, my imagination had been my escape, my friend, and my connection with the world. But as we build our lives, our imaginations can be diminished by the same obligations and responsibilities that rob us of our energy.

While imagination can certainly inspire our passions—literally giving us ideas or showing us the path—it can also be a benefit. Living a Passion-First Life means living with more imagination.

We find that once we do more of the things we love more

consistently, we are kinder to ourselves and more invested in seeing our future ahead of us. We gain confidence to plan adventures, explore alternative careers, or visualize art or businesses that we want to create. You may often hear a Passion Seeker say, "I never would have imagined that I would love this so much!" Until we try the activity or explore the idea, our hearts and minds don't know what it can feel like.

F (Fulfillment)

Take one look at social media, and you'll see many people saying they're "humbled by" or "honored to do" whatever activity they're putting their minds toward. We've all done it, because let's be honest: It's hard to know what language to use to share the things we're proud of, to know the right words to express our gratitude for the opportunity or recognition.

We're reluctant to share when we feel fulfilled, especially when we're doing an activity on our own, just for ourselves. This is understandable, mainly because to some, it may appear selfish to say we're fulfilled. It's almost as if the word *filled* is like the feeling after a celebratory meal, of being stuffed. It's hard to share because fulfillment is incredibly personal. Only you know how passion feels and what fills you up.

Doing more of the things you love becomes fulfilling precisely because you are giving your body and soul what it is craving, what is natural to it. Helping others becomes second nature; and with every outreached hand or every volunteer hour of doing what we love, our passion is nurtured.

E (Energy)

If you're a Passion Seeker, then you're likely looking for "more," but you're asking yourself how you can find the energy to do it.

(There's a reason why the energy drink market is expected to grow to $240 billion by 2027. We are all looking for quick fixes for being WIPED.) We're trying to show up with a smile, a spring in our step, and we're trying to do our best. But most mornings, simply getting out of bed needs multiple alarms!

Doing something you love may require you to work harder than you ever have in your life. You will feel new levels of tiredness that you didn't realize existed. Whether that's launching a side hustle in your downtime or resuming a sport you love, it's *work*. And yet, the energy you gain acts like a fire in your belly, driving you to keep moving forward. And, as academics have proven, pursuing our passions promotes growth in brain health, fitness, flexibility, and confidence, all of which generate positive energy for us and those around us.

What's more, if we know that we have our passions waiting for us, despite the rigors or responsibilities we may be obliged to complete, then the anticipation and confidence of our enjoyment act as beautiful buffers to the hardships we may need to endure.

PART TWO:
SPARKS

What matters is that the passion is yours, and that it is fuel for the stage of life you find yourself in.

Imagine a world where everyone was pursuing their passions 24/7. People are living their DREAMS! No conflict! No famine, war, pain, loss, or suffering! Does that look like a sped-up Benny Hill film (one version of hell, in my opinion) or paradise?

Of course, living our passions constantly and with maximum satisfaction is simply not possible. Life is life; it can be complex and often tragic, unfair, and completely illogical. But between the fantasy of always-on passion and the reality of daily existence lies a more nuanced truth about how passion can fit into our lives.

Tellingly, some of the loudest voices against prioritizing our passions have built profitable careers and personal brands doing exactly that. Simon Sinek, from his position of influence, declares, "People gave me the stupid advice: 'find your passion.' Passion is not the entry point, it's the exit point." Cal Newport, another self-proclaimed "productivity guru," insists that following your passion "not only fails to describe how most people end up with compelling careers but for many people, it can make things worse." Mark Manson bluntly tells us to "Screw Finding Your Passion."

And then there are the influencers, preaching from their mansions, surrounded by their crew, and wearing their $500 sweatpants, telling us that suffering is all in our mind, that it's our reaction to life that is holding us back. That, if we just woke up a little earlier and drank green juice, we'd crush our goals.

Capitalist society thrives on this contradictory message, telling us to both chase our dreams and stay in our lane, to hustle harder but accept our place. People who are pursuing and living their passions can become quite inconvenient in that machine. No wonder, then, that carving out even the tiniest space for doing what we love feels like an act of rebellion.

The real question then becomes: How do we build a life with room for passion? When even the smallest acts—an hour of creative release, a joyful volunteering session—feel like massive undertakings, where do we find our starting point? And how do we keep going?

For Passion Seekers, it isn't about the perfect morning routine or following someone else's blueprint for success. It's about facing why this change feels hard and committing to it anyway. It's about having an anchor to hold on to when the storm is blowing and we're questioning everything, when a Passion-First Life feels a long way away.

We need a new way of thinking and of showing up in the world, of being ourselves despite it all. Modern life will not hand us a thrilling and passionate life; we need to craft it by deciding and claiming what we want, then choosing ever so carefully how we invest ourselves in the world.

I know this is far from easy, especially on the days that feel the hardest, or in times that feel simply too busy to care. So, I've created these "Sparks" to give you that guidance, the permission to acknowledge the challenge, to reach for when you need to get yourself moving—not toward some impossible ideal of constant passion, but toward a life where passion has its rightful place.

Let's begin!

SPARK #1

WE DESERVE IT

I'm going to say something you may not want to hear: that "I Am Enough" mug you bought yourself is holding you back from living the life you want.

You heard me! No mug can replace what you really need—the belief that you deserve more. While accepting ourselves is crucial, the problem with these mugs is that we think that sipping our tea from it is the final step. It's not.

The truth is, we don't need to be convinced we're "enough"—we need to remember who we actually are. Look at what you've already created, overcome, built, and contributed to this world! That's not just "enough"—that's power. Yet somewhere along the way, many of us have forgotten this.

For many Passion Seekers, this disconnect grows over time. Society has a way of slowly dimming our light—through endless expectations, outdated "rules" about who we should be, and messages about staying in our lane. For many facing systemic barriers, discrimination, or marginalization, claiming space in the world requires constant courage. Sometimes telling ourselves we're "enough" becomes a necessary shield, a daily reminder that we deserve to be here.

But here's where it gets tricky. While self-affirmation is important for many of us, it can also become a stopping point. We accept our place and stay within the lines drawn for us. We let the convenient message of being "enough" replace the harder truth: that we deserve more than just enough, that we have the right to grow and to enjoy our lives.

At my speaking engagements, I've hugged attendees who have cried with a mixture of sadness and relief upon realizing their value after years of telling themselves the opposite or ignoring it altogether. At one event, The Pink Chanel Lady (as I call her, due to her fabulous jacket) told me through her tears, "I just realized that I am more than my work." She had forgotten the fullness of who she was, everything she'd built and overcome beyond her job title. Another quietly shared that, on top of her forty-plus-hours-per-week job and thirty-plus hours per week caring for a sick friend, "Maybe, just because I have eleven a.m. to one p.m. free on Saturday, I don't have to volunteer that time to someone else."

There are roles we want to play in life. We are needed by those we care for, and we know we can make a difference, even if that work or activity isn't enjoyable. In fact, it can be mundane, tiring, upsetting, or draining. We know that, but we want to continue dedicating our time and energy to it. The problem appears when we can't see beyond the obligations, responsibilities, and expectations that we carry. Those things become who we are. We forget that we're at our most powerful when we're lit up—creating, contributing, solving, building. That's when we have the most to give to ourselves and others. This includes activities that, on the surface, may have zero productive value, zero connection to work or money, or nothing whatsoever to do with helping the world.

So, it's not that we need to be convinced that we are enough. Every obstacle overcome, every project completed, every person helped, every creative solution found, has proven that time and time again. Instead, we need to remember our strength and uniqueness and believe that we deserve "more"! We are worthy of happiness and fulfillment not despite our flaws, mistakes, and responsibilities, but because of who they make us.

Passion Prompt

Take a moment to reflect on who you truly are in your best moments. When do you feel most like "you"? When do you come alive, express yourself freely, or act in a way that feels completely true? What commitments have you kept, even when they were tough, because they mattered deeply to you?

Now, complete this sentence:

I deserve to pursue my passions because _______________.

Don't rush this. Think about:

* Times you've shown up for others or yourself

* Challenges you've faced and overcome

* Things you've created or built from scratch

* Problems you've solved in your unique way

* Moments when your persistence made the difference

* Ways you've made life better for those around you

Write your statement down and let it settle in. (If it's been a while since you've reminded yourself of your worth, it may take time to get comfortable with this truth.) Keep your "I deserve" statement where you can see it—not just as a reminder of who you are, but as permission to protect the time and energy you need to stay lit up.

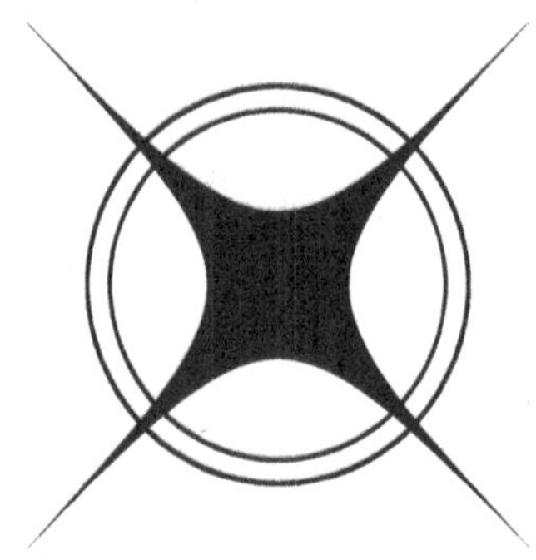

SPARK #2

WE KNOW WHAT WE WANT

Be honest: How many conversations have you had that have gone something like this?

THE OTHER PERSON: What do you fancy for dinner?
YOU: Oh, I don't mind . . .
THE OTHER PERSON: Well, give me a clue! I chose last time!
YOU: Really, I don't mind . . .
THE OTHER PERSON: OK. Let's do burgers!
YOU: No, I don't like burgers!
(And it continues repeating.)

In a world of never-ending choices, we've forgotten how it feels to know what we want, and that's all connected to knowing how we want to feel.

It's not surprising, because ever since childhood, many of us have been taught to focus on collecting accomplishments, rather than how we feel about the life we are experiencing. In an age where "all the feels" is a buzzword (confession: this saying is stuck on my vision board!), where every social media account is sharing every emotion, every step in their day, every ingredient of their trending morning routine or omelet recipe, we are flooded with feelings. Yet, somehow, we're more disconnected than ever from what we truly want.

As parents, we get into the habit of asking everyone else how their day was, of putting everyone else's feelings ahead of our own. As leaders, we have all the best intentions of honoring our team's feelings and desires, but often we are caught between the "rock" of business results and the "hard place" of drinking from a daily fire hose of expectations.

I discovered this disconnect in myself one Saturday morning at my daughter's theater class. She was three or four at the time, and while the morning was frantic getting her there, she loved those classes. One Saturday, I realized that I could, in theory, leave her safely with the teachers and sneak in thirty-five to forty minutes of wandering in the magnificent Minneapolis Institute of Art. The first time I did it, I felt a rush of belonging and beauty, surrounded by art I knew but had forgotten. It was a chance to imagine, to get lost in something, and the art transported me to Europe and my home far away. After that first visit, I knew I wanted more (even if I didn't yet have the words that spoke to the logic of why) so I'd set my timer on my phone and go there while my daughter did her class, staying in the museum until the last possible minute before pick-up time.

A recent study at the Mauritshuis Museum in The Hague has explained that feeling of belonging I experienced. It showed that viewing real-life art activates the precuneus, the part of the brain associated with self-reflection, sense of self, and episodic memories. Erik Scherder, professor of neuropsychology at Vrije Universiteit Amsterdam, explained that "Watching art stimulates your brain on several levels. It evokes excitement, triggers imagination, and makes you think about what you see. It's an ultimate enrichment, activating your brain to the fullest."

I didn't realize how much I desired those feelings of connection until I stole that time on those dance-lesson mornings. As a new parent, I hadn't given myself permission to step away, to do something that filled me up—to claim it for me.

This happens to so many of us. Knowing what we want, let alone saying it out loud, can feel terrifying, because it can be accompanied by a swift realization of *that isn't what I have*. It's a brave act because

it can point us to what is missing in our lives—and that can be a painful exercise, because we are all too aware of the sacrifices, trade-offs, and choices we have made in the decades before that got us to this point.

Let's say that we want more "fire" in our lives. We might not be sure what that fire is, in terms of an activity, but we just want to feel a burning desire for something. That realization can draw us back to the present, where perhaps we're in a relationship that has lost its fizz, a job that bores us, or a role in the household that feels like unbalanced drudgery. Those realizations can give us a stab of panic. We're suddenly confronted by the fact that we have got ourselves so far down a path in life that we cannot turn back.

When we try to get clear about how we want to feel, we may be tempted to instantly self-judge or question, which can stop us in our tracks. And yet, defining how we want our passions to make us feel is an absolutely critical step in exploring them. One of the biggest mistakes I see with Passion Seekers is a good intention of wanting to jump into discovering their passions but not having clarity on what "passion" feels like to them. This either stops them from getting started, or they sign up for every class, every new thing, and burn out FAST.

No one is saying that by seeking more "passion" in your life, you'll suddenly escape the activities that may trigger neutral or negative emotions: the laundry, the spreadsheets, the spouse nagging about the dirty boots, or the exhaustion from the work shift followed by family obligations. This is about you deciding that you want MORE of a certain energy in your life, articulating how that energy feels to you, and being intentional about finding ways to inject more of those feelings into your days, weeks, and months. In fact, if we focus

on the positive emotions that Barbara Fredrickson says "broaden an individual's momentary thought-action repertoire: joy sparks the urge to play, interest sparks the urge to explore, contentment sparks the urge to savor and integrate, and love sparks a recurring cycle of each of these urges," then we begin to find that we are open to more.

In other words, experiencing positive emotions helps us build happier lives. It can also help us reduce stress, build resilience, and improve our overall health. Defining the energy that we want more of helps us filter out how we feel about the new experiences that we do sign up for.

The challenge becomes, after years of delegating our feelings to those of our children, teams, or families, we need to find a new way to access them—and then be brave enough to claim what we want more of. Knowing what we want isn't always an instant "aha"—sometimes it's a slow remembering, an uncovering of desires we'd forgotten or put aside. These desires matter. They guide our choices, give us ideas worth exploring, and show us where to invest our energy. We may not always get exactly what we want, but being clear about it helps us take those first brave steps—even if they're just thirty-five minutes in an art museum.

Passion Prompt

What does passion feel like to you?

* Write down words that describe how you feel when you're doing something you love. Think about moments when time flies, when you experience positive emotions, or when you feel most like yourself.

Examples include *energized, peaceful, brave, curious, satisfied, alive.*

* Which of the feelings that you wrote down do you want more of in your life?
    • Ideally, choose one, but it's fine to pick several.

* Create a new note in your phone, call it "How Passion Feels," write down those words, and continue to do so as you discover and explore activities. While you're on your phone, set a reminder to do a Passion Check-In with yourself regularly; this could be a weekly reflection, or it could be every day with your journaling.
    • Ask yourself, "What activities did I do, or was drawn to, that helped me feel this way? If I'm not feeling it, what else do I need to add or remove from my schedule?"
    • Over time, refine your word list until you have one that you feel describes your passion. My word is "fizzy"!

SPARK #3

WE IGNORE LABELS

Who we think we are, who we truly are, and who the world sees us as are very different things. This confusion of identity can often stop us from trying and pursuing the things we think will light us up.

Remember how Robert Vallerand told us that harmonious passions are defined as activities that have become part of us? This means that instead of just baking cakes on the weekend because you feel like it, you define yourself as a baker. Or maybe you meet Jim at a networking event, and he introduces himself as "the CFO of Acme Construction, and a songwriter."

It makes academic sense that a harmonious passion is one in which we have zero concern about social acceptance and that we incorporate the activity into our lives without any conflict or challenge. However, the world often isn't set up for us in that way.

Identity is both, as the American Psychological Association tells us, "a set of physical, psychological, and interpersonal characteristics that is not wholly shared with any other person," and also "a range of affiliations (e.g., ethnicity) and social roles." We may think we have no choice in the affiliations and roles we've adopted to gain acceptance to a university, build a career, become a parent, or be a community leader. Or we might throw ourselves into those affiliations and roles only to discover, after years of building them, that it's not who we truly are inside.

A common frustration of Passion Seekers is feeling at odds with an identity that has taken years to develop. We crave an authentic way to apply our talents and what we love to our day; we want to feel like "ourselves." The tension comes when we realize we don't know *what* that new identity is! We worry that if we dare try something new, it may damage the identity we've spent our precious energy

creating. This is more than FOPO (fear of people's opinions). This is the terror of vulnerability of admitting our true selves.

We can remove this pressure on ourselves by remembering that identity doesn't need to be singular. For example, William James described identity as having three different dimensions. The first is the "spiritual self": our emotions, values, attitudes, and interests. The second is our "social self," or the way we present ourselves to the outside world and the hats we wear in our lives. And the third is our "material self," or our physical things such as our bodies and possessions.

It's liberating to think about how we can adapt, feed, and grow these different identities at different times in our lives. Some of these identities could be more private (maybe the spiritual one), and others may be more public (the social one).

A brilliant example of someone who embraces multiple identities with their passions is Sir Brian May, best known as Queen's lead guitarist and cofounder. While most of us picture him on stage with the inimitable Freddie Mercury or performing "Bohemian Rhapsody," May's passions extend far beyond music. He holds a PhD in astrophysics, champions animal welfare causes, and is an acclaimed expert in Victorian stereophotography—even receiving the Royal Photographic Society's prestigious Saxby Medal in 2012.

What might seem like an eclectic mix of interests to others is simply Brian pursuing the passions that make his life rich and meaningful. He shows us that we don't need to limit ourselves to just one passion or fit into a single identity. If we wish, we can be many things, contribute and build skills in various areas, and let different passions light us up in different ways.

This freedom to embrace the identity—or identities—we want can be helped by understanding who supports us. Answering two questions can help with this:

1. Who are the people in my life who love me as I am?

2. Who are the ones who want to see me grow and be happy?

During COVID, my passion-first philosophy steered me towards Formula 1. Though I'd grown up with the sport woven into British culture, watching Netflix's *Drive to Survive* turned my past interest into a new fascination. It wasn't long before I was lost in race-day drama, learning statistics, and delighting in the brilliant strategies that unfold behind every pit wall. I had never considered myself an "F1 Fan," but when I reflected upon it, Formula 1 followed threads of values and things I'm drawn to in my life—adventure, courage, strategy and stories.

When I was fresh into this new passion, I had coffee with a business mentor and mentioned that I loved the sport. I still remember his look of scorn as he said, "You? Formula 1?!" Part of this was his disapproval of the conflicted politics (which is fair), but I'm willing to bet that the identity of an auto-racing fan didn't fit my professional, feminine image.

Enter my husband. In 2023, he bought me a surprise birthday gift: tickets to the United States Grand Prix in Austin, Texas. When people asked me what I got from my birthday, I lost count of the people who (again) looked surprised and said, "Why?"

"For fun!" I said (somewhat relishing the look on each person's face, if I'm being honest).

"Fair enough," they shrugged. It was not their idea of a good time, so they couldn't quite understand it.

Let me tell you, to see Sir Lewis Hamilton scream around a corner with Max Verstappen on his tail, to hear the SOUND of those cars, to be cheering at the top of my lungs for every single lap, to experience the sense of belonging with tens of thousands of spectators (many of them are women, by the way!), each wearing the jersey of their favorite driver, was pure exhilaration!

The mix of joy and defiance I feel with my Formula 1 passion is exactly what living a Passion-First Life is all about: discovering what lights us up and finding the courage to pursue it, even when it doesn't align with how others see us, or if the passion itself seems frivolous or meaningless to others.

I've seen similar experiences play out with many Passion Seekers in our community. For them, pursuing a passion isn't just fun, it's an act of courage that challenges expectations about who they "should" be, a following of the voice inside that is telling them to enjoy, to be satisfied, to express themselves.

Think about the people who join spaces where they're the "only one"—the only woman in the coding class, the only person of color in a predominately white business field, the only senior citizen at the skateboard park. Whether these people have tiptoed into these spaces, or jumped right in, they're facing the fact that people may judge them, or single them out for dismissal or discrimination.

Resisting the urge to label ourselves, and instead, embracing who we are—all of the "identities" that make us unique—isn't just about personal fulfillment. Sometimes it's about expanding what's

possible and showing others that they belong in spaces they never imagined themselves. When that voice in your head says "people like me don't do things like that," challenge it. By simply enjoying what you enjoy, without apology, you demonstrate to others that they can do the same. And, when we do our best to ignore the labels, we take another step in living the lives *we* want (and helping others claim theirs, too).

Passion Prompt

Now it's your turn to identify where labels might be holding you back from doing more of the things you love.

* Think of something you've been curious about but haven't pursued. What labels or expectations have held you back?

* Name the people in your life who would support your exploration of a new passion. (Hint: Who accepts and celebrates you for who you truly are?)

* Choose one small action you can take this week to explore an interest without fitting a label. Add it to your weekly plan, do it, then reflect on how it felt.

SPARK #4

WE REFUSE TO BE CONTROLLED BY COMFORT

Pursuing our passions gives us a basic conundrum. We know that finding and maintaining motivation is essential to building the skills needed to pursue an activity that we love or will come to love. Why, then, can it feel so hard to get off the couch, or show up to the class we've signed up for, to learn the thing we were looking forward to learning?

It can help to understand the two main types of motivation that drive us forward and hold us back: extrinsic and intrinsic.

Extrinsic motivation typically involves engaging in behaviors that give us "external incentive to engage in a specific activity, especially motivation arising from the expectation of punishment or reward."

Think of examples like these:

*   Going to the gym to avoid weight gain, and then returning home deflated

*   Attending the work-committee meeting over fears of not looking committed enough, even though the topic sends you to sleep

*   Running the marathon for the medal, swearing during each of the 26.4 miles

*   Wearing the corporate suit to the event to avoid standing out, despite your love of fashion

If you're a high performer, then you've probably generated success mostly due to extrinsic motivation. The rewards can feel soooo

good: the salary increases, the "Employee of the Month" award, giving gifts to those we love … until they don't.

This is the point when Passion Seekers realize that they have relied too much on extrinsic motivation. We literally pour ourselves out in order to gain something we think we *should* have. We know this, and we recognize that we need to do more of what we love to fill us up, but acting on that is an entirely different matter.

Intrinsic motivation should be our friend, but it's by far the less practiced of the two, especially in our lives outside of work. Here's its definition: "an incentive to engage in a specific activity that derives from pleasure in the activity itself rather than because of any external benefits that might be obtained."

So, here's what happens: We reach a point when the lure of extrinsic motivation wears off and intrinsic motivation takes too much energy to muster, due to the baggage of shame that it creates. (How many times have you labelled something you love a "guilty pleasure"?) We let this threat of shame bully us, and we tell ourselves that we're scared to try something new or stop something we don't enjoy.

But, if we're being honest with ourselves, losing our "spark" isn't really about fear. It's about retreating into comfort. When we continually choose our protective bubble, over time, something shifts: Our willingness to try new things shrinks, and our identity becomes more about what we won't do, rather than what we do. We think it's invisible to others; however, our children watch us choose the couch over ourselves. We slowly stop being seen as a role model at work. Our friends stop inviting us to try new things. Our partners learn to expect our "no."

The key isn't waiting to feel brave enough—it's choosing manageable

moments of discomfort on purpose, even when (especially when) we don't feel ready. It's stepping outside on a cold morning, because you know you want to train. It's walking into that work meeting alone and announcing "I'm new here!" before your brain can talk you out of it. It's hitting "publish" on your first blog post, despite your hands shaking. At the time, these moments don't feel particularly brave. In fact, they often feel awkward and inspire grumpiness over joy. But, if we can muster that motivation, it can move us from the "someday" cycle into taking action.

Innovation leader Greg McGee's story shows us what happens when we move beyond extrinsic motivation to find something that lights us up inside. An accomplished professional working in healthcare, Greg rediscovered his passion for creating art during the early days of the pandemic. What started as his daughter's suggestion to help manage stress became a daily practice that has added something special to his life.

"I started creating at least one complete painting or drawing every single day," Greg shares. "Fast forward to today, I have now completed more than two thousand pieces."

Greg posts every piece on his social media pages—"the good, the bad, and the ugly"—using this practice to keep himself accountable. While he's never sold his work, he's given away almost one thousand pieces, spreading joy to others in the process.

Yet even after all this time, Greg still experiences discomfort: "I am still apprehensive and unsure about each piece," Greg admits. "While I know my work has improved, I can see the flaws, and I question the motives. I am certain others will see me as a phony, but I press on. I tell myself that this is a journey of learning and improving."

This journey is a classic case of the desire for competency that is a hallmark of a harmonious passion, and it's created much positivity for Greg and others. "This daily practice has brought me so much good," he reflects. "I've been able to put a few smiles into the world. I've become a better innovator at work. My stress and anxiety are on ice." His commitment has even led to unexpected opportunities, like serving as a Trustee on the Board at the Minneapolis College of Art and Design.

What keeps him pushing past the discomfort? Partly, it's the accountability of sharing each piece—a journey his daughter "gently shoved" him onto. "And I know she is proud of her dad's work," he adds.

No one is saying that this type of determination is easy on our brains, bodies, or egos. Being a beginner or revisiting a hobby or work focus after years may mean that we're behind or prone to making mistakes. We can, quite literally, fall on our faces in front of strangers. (Just ask the people I crashed into while trying cross-country skiing in a fit of lockdown-induced exploration. I can now categorically state that cross-country skiing, after this and other attempts, is not a passion I have any motivation to pursue! At least I now know what I'm willing to feel uncomfortable for—and what I'm not!)

One of the hardest things we can do is reset our relationship with comfort—we think it protects us, when at best it's holding us back, and at worst, it might be harming our happiness and fulfillment. Like any habit we need to break, we must start with being honest with how comfort is showing up in our lives. Does it nourish— through rest and restoration—or keep us stuck? (That evening bath that helps you recharge? Keep it. Spending hours scrolling in your

fantasy football app instead of joining the guys in a kick-about game? That's not comfort—that's retreat.)

This isn't about relinquishing *all* comfort in your life. Think of it more like dialing your reliance back and willing yourself to embrace a little more temporary discomfort so that, eventually, you get to experience the positive benefits that pursuing your passion will bring.

And, if you find yourself hesitating or feeling fearful, remember the advice that stand-up comedian Trish Cook once shared at a Passion Collective event, "If it all goes wrong, you've got a great story to tell!"

Passion Prompt

Our relationship with comfort can be a fine balance to manage. Reflect on these questions to explore where you find yourself with it:

* What "comfort" is restorative for you, and what is retreat?

* If you have an activity that you describe as a "guilty pleasure" why do you describe it that way?

* Is there an activity you want to try, but are hesitating to do so because it feels uncomfortable? Name that discomfort.

* What would make this discomfort worth it? What could be waiting on the other side?

SPARK #5

WE FUEL OURSELVES

In 2007, a study by economist Alan Krueger claimed that we're only spending 20 percent of our time on things that are meaningful to us, everything from spiritual practice to talking with close friends.

That's 1.4 days in our week that we're devoting to activities that are filling us up. This fascinated me. Is this realistic, given our modern lives? Or woefully inadequate?

When I explored this further, it got interesting. Krueger learned that in the last fifty years, the "share of time devoted to 'mundane chores' such as ironing has decreased, while time spent on 'neutral downtime' activities, such as watching television has increased."

Both male and female survey respondents were spending far less time in their day reading books and performing paid work. (Yes, really. Less time, not more.) Men were spending more time "relaxing and doing nothing" in 2005 than women (!) and much more time on "crafts," yet the percentage of the day in which both genders engaged in "artistic activity" was down—to 0.02 of the day for women and a flat 0.00 for men.

Surprising, isn't it? It prompted me to think—is our inability to pursue our passions about being starved of time, or is it how we're spending that time?

Have you ever gone to a gathering you think you should attend, trying to belong, feeling for a connection? "I should do this," you tell yourself. And if you didn't participate, what if you missed out on friendship? Or information? What if people thought less of you for your absence?

You leave the event, your energy zapped, knowing the event has created emptiness over fulfillment. The next time the invitation comes, your finger hovers over the RSVP button. Do you go, without a guarantee that it will give you what you need?

Brené Brown tells us that choices should either be a "F*** yeah!" or not at all. Brené, I love you, but it's not that easy. This clarity requires us to get familiar with missing out, not being invited, losing money, or being seen as standoffish, boring, or weird. It demands that we know ourselves and our preferences deeply enough to opt out and still know that we're a good person who has something to offer, even if others don't see it.

Kreuger's "meaningful time" study was published the same year that the iPhone was launched, so it doesn't include the time spent on our devices, social media, or watching streaming entertainment. Reports vary, but it's safe to say that we spend anywhere from two to three hours of our day on social media and the same for streaming TV. This, by basic math, adds up to more than a month every year. A month, just on social media. Let that sink in! How does that make you feel? (I can tell you; I had to check the math because it shocked me so much.)

While there are some undoubtable benefits that these technologies have brought to us, there's also plenty of evidence to prove that they are damaging our relationships, mental health, and even our eyesight. We all know this. However, instead of protecting the precious commodity of time, we waste it through the self-sabotage of doomscrolling or Netflix marathons.

It's easy to blame our lack of passion on not having enough time, but the truth is harder to admit. It can feel safer to spend hours on Instagram, judging others who are pursuing their passions, rather

than devoting time to our own. After all, passive consumption asks nothing of us—we don't have to fail at anything new. Instead, we can comment on other people's efforts, finding a false sense of agency in lives we may feel increasingly disconnected from. This consumption is not only draining our time, but it's sapping the very energy we need to pursue our passions in the first place.

To live a Passion-First Life, we need to fuel ourselves differently—not just to begin, but to sustain our journey. Our passions give us the gift of pushing ourselves. They demand that we enjoy our lives, living with intention, blocking distractions, and remembering what's important. They ask more of us, challenging us physically and emotionally. Once we start pursuing our passions, the work intensifies. We're building the website after doing the dishes, learning new skills over lunch, contributing to the after-hours work committee, assuaging self-doubt, ideating, and believing.

This all takes time and energy—plenty of it—and the risk is that we, ironically, burn out as we pursue the things we love. If you truly want to live a Passion-First Life, you'll need to actively build energy, inspiration, and courage—all in the same twenty-four hours each day that you had before.

Think of this as building FIRE inside yourself. What activities will inspire and strengthen you? If you reallocated your weekly ten hours of social media to this, how would you invest it?

Here's a framework to help you imagine what that could look like for you.

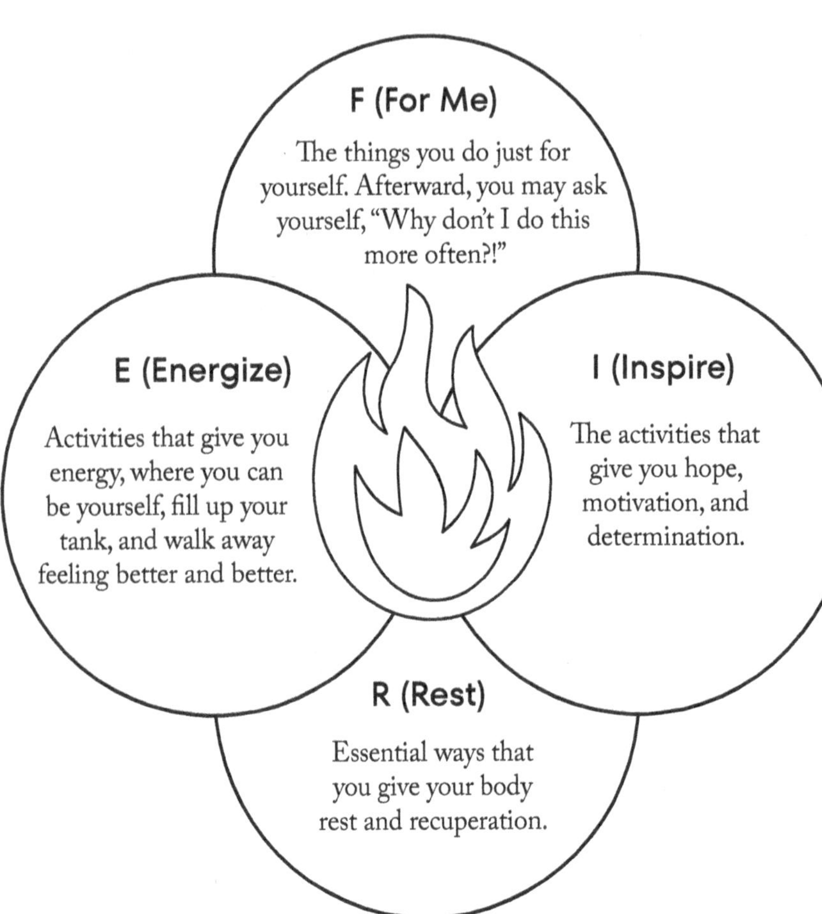

F (For Me)
The things you do just for yourself. Afterward, you may ask yourself, "Why don't I do this more often?!"

E (Energize)
Activities that give you energy, where you can be yourself, fill up your tank, and walk away feeling better and better.

I (Inspire)
The activities that give you hope, motivation, and determination.

R (Rest)
Essential ways that you give your body rest and recuperation.

Passion Prompt

Take these steps to help yourself reflect on, and adapt, your self-care practices:

* Track your time for one typical day (be honest!)
    * How much time goes to passive consumption (social media, streaming, etc.)?
    * How much time goes to activities that inspire or strengthen you?

* Review the FIRE framework and ask yourself:
    * Which category needs the most attention right now?
    * What is one activity that you could add in that category?
    * What might you need to say no to in order to make space for this?

SPARK #6

WE FIND
OUR PEOPLE

There's a certain type of loneliness that appears when you're distant from your passions. It is an aching pain that can creep up on you when you least expect it. There you go, living the life that you'd planned, checking the success boxes you have given yourself (and that others may have given you), and—*BOOM!* It hits you.

It's a feeling of disconnection, of going through the motions, of smiling through it or saying "Yes, boss" when you feel the least like it.

It's a curious sensation of slipping back down a slope ever so slowly, trying to hang on with your fingernails to a life you thought you wanted. A life others may have sacrificed to give you and one that you are grateful to have.

You are following one path, you are in one job (maybe even holding down two), you are spending your time in a certain way, and you know it's not for you. You begin to admit that it's not lighting you up; and that you can be better and do better for yourself and others. Sometimes this feeling of "better" or "more" runs in direct opposition to your goals or what you promised others you'd provide.

Most of all, this disconnection makes you feel empty.

In 2023, the US Surgeon General declared a new public health epidemic: loneliness. He shared that loneliness has the same negative health impact as smoking fifteen cigarettes a day, increasing the risk of premature death by nearly 30 percent. It's hard to reconcile the invisibility of loneliness with the black tar of a cigarette, gray ash dropping on the floor. But that sinking ache is a complex sensation that many of us know.

Loneliness is a tricky enemy because it creates such self-doubt that we feel forced to strap on the armor that stops us from putting ourselves out there. We know that to be less lonely means to meet more like-minded people. However, that fear of not belonging, of walking alone into a room of strangers, praying that our hope of friendship, connection, and passion isn't disappointed, can be the very reason we don't make the leap.

The antidotes to loneliness—connection and belonging—look and feel different for every individual. Kristi Jacobson, a senior financial services leader, told me about her surprising approach over coffee. At a Passion Collective event, she'd casually mentioned that one of her passions was water-skiing (show skiing, the one with human pyramids!). I was intrigued about how Kristi had found it and what it gave her. So, when we had coffee a few weeks later, I asked her, "Water-skiing?! Tell me more!"

Tears spilled down Kristi's face.

I was horrified. I'd made Kristi cry! Immediately, I apologized, and she grasped my hand and told me that her beloved aunt used to be a brilliant water-skier. After her aunt had passed away, Kristi had wanted to feel closer to the woman she had loved so much, so she'd decided to visit a local water ski club she'd found on Google.

Kristi had shown up there—alone. And she still remembered how she felt on that first day.

"I totally identify as an introvert," she said. "Even in a professional setting, going into a crowd of people where I don't know anyone is so outside of my comfort zone. The first memory I have of that day is looking down that hill, at everyone who knows each other,

and thinking, *Oh boy! What have I done?* But I did it. There it was. I couldn't turn around then!"

This community helped Kristi do things she had never imagined doing, including dressing up in spandex and performing complex "ballet ski" moves in front of crowds, even on the coldest of Minnesota days.

"When I joined the team," she explained, "it was during a really hard time for our family. When I went to the show site every day, I had this great escape from everything else that was going on. I had [the younger water-skiers] run up to give me a big hug and jump into my arms. They were so excited to see me! That was part of that community, too, that I really needed. It created some joy for me that I will be able to carry on after my kids [have left home], that I will have something for myself that I can really immerse myself into and continue to have those friendships, that community—something fun for me."

This story proves how community can be an antidote to loneliness through the harmonious passions it helps us to create. Kristi experienced the connection (or relatedness) to her aunt and to others. She also developed "competence," which motivated her continued learning, and she relished the autonomy of a sport that couldn't be more different from her day job.

Above all, Kristi *found her people.* The team welcomed her without hesitation and lifted her up—literally. If she'd never taken that deep breath and walked down the hill with her life jacket on that first day, she never would have experienced the camaraderie and shared experience that is now such an important part of her life.

Passion Prompt

Think of the people you need in your life, for example: champions, supporters, healers, inspirers.

* What people do you think you need more of in your life?

* When has a community helped you become more of who you are?

* Are you holding back on pursuing something because you don't want to do it alone? If your answer is yes, what would help you make that move?

SPARK #7

WE TRANSFORM OUR SHAME STORIES

As a young girl, I was an avid reader. I loved *Choose Your Own Adventure* books, where you got to decide whether your character jumped into a cave, turned onto the dark road, or sailed across an ocean. I loved the romances, the histories, the friendship stories—anything that would give me escape and a sense of connection to another world. I read most of my books through my town's library, but my bibliophile Mum also made sure they were in my Christmas stockings.

At the grand old age of ten, I decided to start a business. It was called "Laura's Library." I would take a bag of my books to school and lend them to my friends for a small fee. I even created those cute library cards, complete with a Laura's Library logo, and would place them carefully into each of my beloved books, ready for my reader to "check out."

Business boomed from day one. My friends flocked to Laura's Library during lunch break, and I was so happy that I was sharing what I loved—and that I had earned some pennies for the sweet shop and my *Smash Hits* magazines!

After a few days, my parents received a stern call from the school's headmaster. Apparently, one of my friend's parents had reported me for setting up a business at school. I remember Mum and Dad being rather bemused, but they were not given a choice: I had to immediately shut down "Laura's Library."

I now chuckle at my entrepreneurial spirit and hard work to offer what clearly was a valuable service to willing customers. And yet, forty years on, I also remember the sting of shame. I had done something "wrong." I had been trying to take advantage of my friends, to trick people, to overstep my bounds. At least, that was what I'd heard.

Why didn't my friend's parent just send my parents a private note? Why did it feel so bad? Why did I feel like I'd let so many people down? Because shame was being used to control me. Shame, which Brené Brown has categorized as "the intensely painful feeling or experience of believing that we are flawed and therefore unworthy of love and belonging," is a powerful force to deploy.

Shame is society's time-tested way for putting us in our place, and this was my first taste of feeling Whac-a-Moled into conformity. Sure, I had broken an unwritten school rule, but the response to my entrepreneurial self-expression left such a vivid mark that it contributed to me becoming a dedicated rule-follower and people pleaser for years to come. These learned behavioral traits worked a treat, helping me through the 1980s and 1990s education system and into a top job. They also enabled my climb up the corporate ladder—until they didn't anymore, and I realized I was pleasing the wrong people for the wrong reasons. All for fear of shame.

I now wonder how this experience influenced my development, and what opportunities I didn't explore because of it. I wonder what it told me about my worth and the contribution I could make to a community. I wonder how it affected my relationship with money.

I bet that you also have experiences where you acted upon a passion—something that you loved, without maybe knowing why—and you were made to feel shame about it. Enough shame that you stopped it and perhaps never picked it up again.

Overcoming this shame residue isn't easy, and it can certainly get in the way of trying new things as we explore potential passions.

It's not easy to invest money in your passion if you have financial trauma from your childhood.

It's not easy to try a new sport if you were always the last to be chosen for the team.

It's not easy to start a business if you were told it was wrong to ask people for money.

It's not easy to fight for a cause you believe in if you were told to be a "good girl."

It's not easy to express yourself creatively if you were taught that it didn't make you "man enough."

The list is endless, and I certainly don't have the silver bullet to solve shame. (See Brené for that!) However, what I do know is that when I reflect on my "Laura's Library" experience, I recognize themes. I see myself creating community, writing this book, sharing what I love, and helping people feel the same energy. That spark in ten-year-old me didn't die; I just had to find the right vehicle and the right chapter in my life for it.

Past passions—even those silenced by shame—can show us the best part of ourselves. Sometimes it just takes time and courage to claim them.

Passion Prompt

Ask yourself the following questions:

* Do you have an experience from your past where you acted on a passion and then felt shame about it? What was it?

* Looking back, did this change anything about your path? Did you act differently? Or make different decisions?

* What stories are you still telling yourself from that experience that are not true?

WE CRAFT OUR JOBS

Born to Buzz

I was once told by an HR leader that we should expect to actively dislike 30 percent of our job. I'm not talking a shoulder shrug or a meeting-doze here. I'm talking *dislike.*

The HR leader's desire to help was tempered with a resigned demeanor. To my ears, this advice sounded like, "Suck it up, buttercup. You want the maybe-you'll-get-it-maybe-you-won't year-end bonus? Throw on that armor, and get on with the grind! Giddyup!"

I knew in that moment that the job they wanted me to rededicate myself to (and the culture they were mandating, which was moving swiftly away from my values), was not one I could commit myself to. Thirty percent of my week was not something I wanted to feel "less than" for. (I did the proper math afterward: Thirty percent of your job is seventy-two days every year. *Seventy-two days!*)

When we can leave these cultures, as I did, it can give us clarity— and a new start. But what happens when we don't want to quit our job? What if we simply do not have the option to leave?

A first step is *job crafting*, a concept that "captures what employees do to redesign their own jobs in ways that can foster job satisfaction, as well as engagement, resilience, and thriving at work."

While this may sound like organized chaos, it also makes sense. We apply for job descriptions that have been written (often hastily or with corporate templates) based on a hiring leader's best idea of the business needs at that time. Once we spend time in that role as a human with other humans, living through life's challenges and highlights, growing, learning, and making mistakes, it's only logical that either we or our jobs need to evolve.

Historically, we've been told that *we* have to change (just like that HR leader told me), but job crafting gives us another option: shape the job to us.

The examples of job crafting are endless: the housekeeping staff who create competitions for the number of beds changed; the sous-chef who subs for the patisserie section on his days off; the IT supervisor who creates a mentoring program for up-and-coming coders; the gym trainer who integrates ballet into his classes, just because he loves it.

I saw this for myself one November day, as I flew between Knoxville, Tennessee, and Atlanta, Georgia, after attending a conference. It was one of those tiny planes where you typically spend more time figuring out how to fold yourself into the seat than expecting anything but a basic flight. I couldn't have been more wrong. In stepped our flight attendant—a tall woman with a blonde bob and a presence that transformed our cramped cabin into something more akin to a Waldorf Astoria hotel.

She welcomed us with genuine delight, sharing that at seventy-five years old, she was living her childhood dream. When she offered the snack service, she presented each item as if it was the best thing you'd eat all week. Even as she demonstrated the safety instructions, she made it her own, like a show for us all. This wasn't just someone doing their job—this was Trudy, creating magic in every interaction, radiating joy as if there was nowhere else in the world she'd rather be.

I asked her for a photo, and later we exchanged texts. In one, I asked her why being a flight attendant was her passion, and she told me: "At a very early age, growing up the eldest of five in a

very abusive childhood, creating in me an overwhelming sense of shame . . . I decided to show the world that I was better than what I came from. I decided—early on—to be the BEST of whatever I became." Her alcoholic parents, she told me, taught her mainly "how not to be," but Trudy told me her alcoholic parents taught her mainly "how not to be," but she used this experience as fuel. At thirty, she pursued her college degree, spending twelve years earning her business degree with honors. She didn't stop there—adding two graduate degrees and a career as a business analyst at an airline. Then, at fifty, she made one final attempt at her childhood dream of becoming a flight attendant. "It was the absolute happiest day of my life when the airline said 'YES!'" she shared. "I had the privilege of living my dream that made me the happiest! And even today, I love my job and my life and feel very proud of who and what I've become."

Trudy was crafting her job right there, in front of us. She was determined to make our day, to make us feel special. I am sure she has said those words a million times, often to people who, at best, barely make eye contact with her. She was transforming the shame stories from her past, and using her innate talents and personality to make the job her own. She was pure, inspirational panache!

While job crafting can make your current role more satisfying, enjoyable, and aligned with who you are, it can also open up an entirely new career direction.

Astrid Benedetto's story shows us how. As a senior diversity, equity, and inclusion (DEI) leader, Astrid began her journey differently. After being laid off from her finance role at Target, she reflected on her path ahead. She realized that she'd started a career in finance to capitalize on her analytical skills, and to "(be) an obedient child, going with what my parents influenced. I have this great analytical mindset; however, there's always something that I feel like I'm missing."

What emerged for Astrid was a common career thread of helping others reach their potential. This was informed by her lived experience growing up in a minority ethnic group in Indonesia and experiencing discrimination from the government and the native peoples.

At Target, Astrid had participated in the Asian Business Council and begun to connect the dots to the new career she wanted: a leadership role in DEI. She had one major obstacle, though: DEI is a highly competitive discipline, and if she wanted to pivot her career, she'd be competing with candidates with heavy public-sector experience.

For some, this may have been discouraging. But Astrid doubled down on her efforts and determinedly sought out companies who had admirable, authentic DEI strategies. She said, "The layoff provided me with an opportunity to find my purpose and recenter my career, drawing from my lived experiences and also growing up with prejudice and discrimination to recenter my work on inclusion and equity."

Instead of applying immediately for roles, Astrid secured a role as a corporate auditor at a leading US bank, communicating her passion with her leader as part of her interview process. She began proactively sharing content with her corporate audit team and joined the Asian Business Resource Group in a leadership position. When she applied, she once again raised her hand to the DEI leader, mentioning that if there was any opportunity to join the team, she'd love to know more. A month later, the same leader shared that a position had opened up, and that she wanted Astrid to join despite

her finance background. Astrid applied, with the blessing of her then-current leader, and got the job.

What does this show? Patience. Determination. Clarity. Self-belief. And a compassionate boss who saw her direct report's passion as a positive.

Astrid didn't just craft an existing job; she pivoted her career. But, as she says, "you do not need a formal title of DEI to do inclusion work. You can start influencing inclusion and belonging in the space that you are in. You also do not need to be a people leader to influence the work."

To be successful at job crafting, you'll need some key elements in place:

* A description of your passion and how it may help your organization's goals.

* Willingness to add your extra "passion" activities to your existing responsibilities.

* A plan for how to balance any extra work with your health (e.g., keeping time for family, nutrition, and exercise).

* Above all, a trusting relationship with your leader where they have proven that they care for your career development and personal happiness.

When these elements align, job crafting can give you space to practice your passions, and even open doors you might never have imagined.

Passion Prompt

If you're looking to gain more meaning from your existing job through "crafting," or if you're looking to change your path entirely, ask yourself these questions:

* What is your life experience telling you about where to spend your extra time?

* Where do you see the opportunity to contribute your talents to the organization, regardless of your job title?

* How much capacity do you have in your work week? (Be honest with yourself. If it's an hour, let it be an hour, and start there.)

SPARK #9

WE LET GO OF CERTAINTY

We're all hardwired to seek certainty, to look for guaranteed outcomes. Yet, for us to live a Passion-First Life we need to step beyond what feels safe and predictable.

A paycheck is security. It (hopefully) keeps us on top of our bills; and if we're lucky, it gives us fun money to do more of the things we love to do. Family, or our inner circle, can feel like certainty because they've known us for so long. The recurring, reliable schedule of our jobs can give us a routine that our brains, bodies, and families may need. We want to be sure that people will accept and acknowledge us, because that's how we've built our careers and lives so far.

However, "certainty" is an illusion, and it's often one of the biggest reasons why people don't do more of what they love in work and life. Let's start with work. To paraphrase Maya Angelou, if you like yourself, what you do, and how you do it, then you're in a good position to claim that your job is enhancing your life. When it works, your job enables you to do more of what you love—funding the trips you cherish, paying for those fitness training sessions, or building the network for your nonprofit work. This interconnection can be profound and powerful.

But if your job is, more often than not, harming your health, or causing you to "flatline" as I did, if you dislike the values, ethics, or processes of your company, or, in the worst case, if your job is turning you into a different person—then no, that "certainty" of that particular paycheck or career path is not worth it.

My good friend Sebastian's journey shows us how certainty isn't always a gift. As a finance professional, he had spent years working hard and was poised for a promotion—his boss was leaving, and everyone

assumed he'd step into her role. Even better, *her* boss was approaching retirement, creating a clear path to an even higher position.

For many, this career certainty would be a dream. But Sebastian saw something different: The higher he climbed, the less time he spent on the intellectual work he loved, replaced instead by endless management meetings. He realized that the money that was being offered, as grateful as he was for the promise of it, couldn't compensate for spending his days in ways he didn't enjoy. Sebastian began to explore alternative scenarios, such as consulting, living with family members for periods of time, or even relocating to countries with lower living costs. "Once I had 'done the math' and was able to clearly see that I would never be homeless or go hungry," he explains, "making choices that would allow me to focus on spending my career time in ways that I enjoy became easier."

We often tell ourselves that certainty means security, and in chasing it, we forget to ask ourselves what price we are willing to pay for it. Sebastian's choice shows us that trade-offs do exist. "They call it a career ladder, and built into that is a presumption that one must climb as high as one can. I have found that being in the middle of the proverbial ladder is actually quite rewarding—it provides me with ample financial security while allowing me do work that makes me happy and also provides more free time and flexibility for the things I enjoy outside of work."

When it comes to hobbies or starting a side hustle, the role of certainty can be just as complicated. For example, sharing something we've poured our heart into, especially if we're not an expert at it, can be an incredibly vulnerable experience—and there is no certainty in the result. Starting a business may give no guarantee of the outward symbols of success you either once had or previously thought you could achieve. Beginning an art project or signing up

for a challenge may give us the hope of certainty with creating or finishing something, yet we don't know what that painting will look like—or if we'll finish the marathon standing up!

Our grip on certainty can freeze us in place. We tell ourselves that we can just put up with it for another year, just to get to bonus time or to that promotion. That we'll just work later at night to catch up or turn a blind eye to the dubious management practices that we witness (or, worse, are being asked to execute). Or, we add another interest to our never-ending "Bucket List," waiting for enough time to begin.

What can help is shifting from the word *certainty* as a solitary concept, as a noun. Instead, looking at *what* we can be *certain* about (more like a verb) can help us regain control and decide what we're willing to invest in or sacrifice.

Let's say you've got some opinions about a topic that matters to you and that you think will help other people, and you're considering starting a blog. The uncertainty of how people will react, or what they will think, can be paralyzing. The uncertainty of knowing how to design or launch a blog can also be unnerving, especially if you're skilled at your day job. But what you can be certain about is your expertise in this topic, your genuine desire to help others, and your proven ability to learn new skills when they matter to you.

Or maybe you're unfulfilled in your work and you're considering talking with your leader. You worry about sharing the work you want to do more of because there's a risk that they may think you're disloyal. Instead of assuming that there are no options for you, use your certainty about your track record of contributions, your clear vision for how you could add more value, and your ability and determination to grow.

You have certainty; it's just living in a different place. It's living in your capability to create alternatives, and in your supportive network of friends and family. It's living in the belief that even if you fail, you will have absolute certainty that you've given it the best shot possible. It's your courage to be willing to have that tough conversation with your boss and come to the table with ideas on how you can contribute differently at work, maybe to everyone's benefit.

What is your certainty?

Passion Prompt

* Is there something you classify as "certainty" in your life that, if you're being honest, is more of a crutch?

* What can you be certain about in your life that has nothing to do with work?

* Is your desire for certainty about an outcome holding you back from doing something you might love?

SPARK #10

WE PROUDLY DABBLE

If I were to ask you today, "What are your interests?" would you be able to tell me the answer?

Back in 2014, I wouldn't have known how to respond other than, "My family . . .?" I was running so hard, giving myself zero time to contemplate—let alone pursue—the things I loved. I didn't realize that those interests weren't dead; they were simply hidden beneath the rush and pressure of daily life.

Interests are like pacesetters for our passions—or, put another way, they're the warm-up act. These are activities or experiences that we are curious about, that we may engage in or consume passively and intermittently. But in our chase for success, and in the constant rush of our days, these natural parts of life get squeezed out until we can barely remember what used to light us up.

Why is it hard to develop interests in the first place? Well, today's culture of swiping and instant judgment is training us to, in a split second, shut others down when we see them sharing their opinions, creativity, accomplishments, or the dog joke that made them laugh. We're so quick to swipe past others that it's not surprising we don't give ourselves room to explore.

What we've lost—and what we need to regain—is what expert Todd Kashdan calls *joyous exploration*, which he defines as "the prototype of curiosity—the recognition and desire to seek out new knowledge and information, and the subsequent joy of learning and growing." Joyous exploration is a key ingredient of the conditions, environment, and mind space that we need to pursue things we think we may love in the first place.

Joyous exploration sounds wonderful in theory. But if you've been awake since 4 a.m. doing three loads of laundry before the school run, or you're stuck behind the same desk all day, the idea of curiously exploring *anything* feels laughably out of reach. And while companies promote curiosity as a corporate value, the reality of employees questioning and exploring often creates too much disruption to be welcome. We need a path to curiosity that is more realistic, more doable—something that fits into the corners of our busy lives.

Enter a wonderful word: ***dabbling***.

Its official definition is "a superficial or intermittent interest, investigation, or experiment." Ouch! Even the dictionary makes it sound cold—I prefer the more casual definition of "to dip a little and often," originating from sixteenth-century English. Now that sounds like fun!

Dabbling is doing something you enjoy simply *because*. It's doing it without worry of outcome, judgment, or success. It's messy. It's incorrect. It gives us a chance to start and stop, to experiment, to leave things unfinished if need be. What's more, dabbling can help us develop interests, which then turn into passions. Here are some examples:

* Spending time on the lake gives you the confidence to learn how to fish, and after a few summers, you begin competing.

* Volunteering for the committee at work gives you visibility and experience in an activity or discipline that isn't part of your job description.

* You finally get your cello out of the attic and begin to futz

around with it. After a while, you remember how it feels to play the cello, and before long, you've joined a local string quartet that plays just for themselves.

If we were to dabble more, we'd literally get our hands dirty with trying and making progress whenever we had the time.

As children, we are often encouraged or educated with several activities because science has shown this helps our long-term development. Famous sports stars often played multiple sports until they found their true focus. At their respective high schools, US National Soccer Hall of Famer Abby Wambach was an accomplished basketball player, and basketball icon LeBron James was a sought-after football wide receiver!

However, for most of us who aren't world-class athletes, as we become adults, this idea of dabbling gets lost. The pressure to succeed and get recognition for our accomplishments, as well as our dramatically increased lack of time, stops us from simply trying stuff out.

Even the concept of dabbling can be paired with shame. Dabbling sounds alchemic, risky, frivolous, dangerous, noncommittal. You might find yourself saying you "dabble" in something with a shrug and a lowered head, suggesting, *It's not important. It's silly. I know it's not as good as it could be.*

We say this because we are afraid to admit we're not an expert. We may have a fixed mindset, a full calendar, or a lack of deliberate practice, instruction, or patience to improve it.

But the truth is, dabbling is a perfect way of experimenting and

feeling out if we want an interest to become a passion. Take my interest in my family's history, for instance. I adore diving down the Ancestry.com rabbit hole, discovering and exploring the people in my family, their connections and lives.

Some people may say that to truly get the most out of this activity, I "should" write a book about the characters and connections I'm discovering, complete the family tree, or travel to Canada to visit the graves of my great-great-uncles, who were World War I heroes. And yet, I don't do these things. Not because I don't want to, but because I don't need to. . . yet. I enjoy my dabbling, my "mooching around," my rabbit-holing. Perhaps I don't want to get too serious about this interest—yet.

Perhaps the whole reason that I love this activity is that it's NOT finish-able. That it's something I can continue returning to, a source of comfort, aspiration, and progress. That the *yet* gives me something I can look forward to.

Does it make it any less valuable because I'm not a fully paid-up member of the National Genealogical Society, spending my days in dusty archives? That my activities could be seen by those experts as aimless?

No. It's not about the frequency, the duration, or the qualification level of my interest. It's how it makes me—and us—feel. We should hold on to that feeling, nurture it, and use it to *fuel* our passions.

Passion Prompt

* What interests, other than family, do you have?

* What holds you back from dabbling more often (e.g., making a mess)?

* What obligation could you let go of, or delegate in the next month, to give yourself time to dabble?

SPARK #11

WE REACH BACK TO MOVE FORWARD

When we realize we want "more" in life, it should, in theory, feel good to admit that we have new opportunities and adventures ahead of us. But often, it can feel overwhelming, and we tell ourselves that we don't know where to start, and that we have no ideas for what we'd do to get that "extra" that we are craving. Of course, it's not that we've suddenly become an empty vessel (even if it feels like it on our most stressful days). What happens is that we get so caught up in our routines of performing, leading, and serving others that we lose our imagination for how our days might be different.

The best way to fire up that imagination is not always to look ahead, even if that feels like the most natural thing to do. We have a powerful resource, right there inside of us, that gives us clues to what may light us up in the future—our life experiences. Yet, we often avoid looking back, whether that's due to shame, pain, or simply a desire to keep moving on. We all have moments that need to stay firmly in the past (ask any Gen X-er why we're *very* glad the memories of our youth are not on Facebook!) but when we look at our history differently, we can find hidden beauty.

Instead of blocking or running from our past, it can help to imagine ourselves as gold prospectors, sifting through our experiences to evaluate what they meant to us and what we can carry forward into activities that light us up in our *future*.

We don't need to relive or resurrect things that we no longer love or feel an affinity for (particularly those activities that could be harmful to us). Instead, let that sand and dirt fall through the sieve and be washed away. Then ask yourself, "How can I focus my energy on finding the gems?"

Reaching back can remind us of our past strengths and talents. We

remember the obstacles we overcame, the tenacity we showed, the creativity that shone when we let it, and the courage we showed when we let ourselves leap. We begin to believe that the passions might not be dead inside us, that they may simply be waiting to be reawakened or reworked into something that fits who we are—and what we need—today.

One way to access these memories is to remember the reasons why you loved an activity in the first place. These could be memories of warmth, pride, or delight; or undisputable, hard-fought accomplishments that you carved out due to your passion for the topic or goal you were chasing down. Connecting the dots in this way can move us beyond point-in-time moments (e.g., a job title at a certain company, a chapter in your life that you left long ago) to the experience that gave us the feeling that we are trying to rediscover.

Recently, I found myself remembering an experience from more than fifteen years ago. Back then, I was a director at a Fortune 500 company, and our team won the Chairman's Award for Dream Book, a tool that helped people imagine and plan their dream retirement. While the crystal award on my desk marked a career milestone, what stands out now are the passions woven through that project: books, imagination, helping people live their best lives, community, stories, and playing the system to win. These same themes light me up today, years later. Yet, this realization doesn't mean that I need to return to corporate financial services to find meaningful work. It tells me that I can take those themes and weave them into my work today, leaving behind what's less desirable for me now, in this stage of life.

This can also apply to our leisure time. Let's say that you used to love skiing, but now you can't imagine yourself bombing down steep

slopes in the freezing cold. Instead of relegating that activity to the past, try to remember the things associated with it that you loved to give you clues about why that activity lit you up. Those clues can help you imagine ways that you can rediscover those feelings in a way that fits your current chapter of life.

Those clues could look like this:

* **Clue:** The sense of freedom and adventure you felt when skiing down the hill
    * **Idea:** If your knees won't take a ski run, what outdoor activity might give you the same feelings, but in a different way?

* **Clue:** The feeling of being a strong, healthy human outside of a gym
    * **Idea:** What fitness activity or challenge would energize you in this chapter of life?

* **Clue:** You remember the joy of helping the kids in the ski school
    * **Idea:** Would mentoring others in something you love (and have skill in) light you up?

Mining our past for clues about our passions can also give us inspiration when we're faced with challenges. When Junita Flowers found herself in a situation marred by domestic violence, she experienced her "rock bottom" while stranded on the shoulder of a freeway, frozen about which direction to take in her life. After that day, she knew she was the only person who could elevate herself from her situation.

To do that, she returned to her past to gain comfort and, most importantly, hope.

"As a child in a big family," Junita said, "I spent a lot of time in the kitchen with my mom and grandmother. That's where my best memories of childhood were shaped, formed, and experienced, and the memories were mine. When I was looking for something that belonged to me, I started baking again. The more I baked, the more memories came up. It was a happy place in the midst of chaos. And then I started doing it for other people, and eventually they started requesting it. It's just what I knew. Baking helped me connect with those memories and find an escape that allowed me to cope."

Junita used these memories—the GOOD things—to help fuel her to get out of the worst period of her life and begin her business. Junita's Jar now makes cookies that are sold across the US, including select Target stores; and Junita is only just beginning.

Passion Prompt

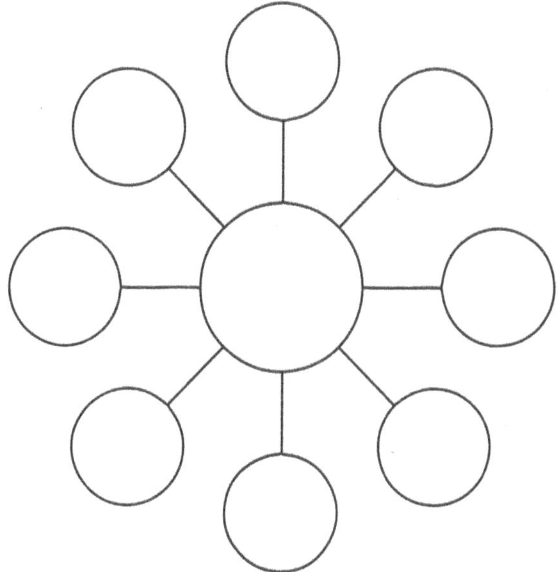

1. Choose a past activity that used to light you up and write that down in the middle circle.

2. Add the associated feelings or experiences into the circles around it. Note those bright sparks that come into your memory. These can be your feelings, or even scents and sounds. Don't try too hard to shape them; just write them down. Add as many connectors and circles as you want—don't be afraid to get messy or to make this your own!

3. Reflect on what you see. Is the activity something you want to pick up as is? Or adapt for where you are in your life now?

SPARK #12

WE ARE RELENTLESSLY RESOURCEFUL

Once we have a clear sense for what we want to do more of, an intimidation factor can creep into our hearts and minds. Often, it can feel like there is only one path to pursue—one way to execute the idea or generate the energy we're craving.

Let's say you're a project manager who has rediscovered the pleasure and sophistication of wine. You've become fascinated with it, beyond simply having a tipple with your friends on a Friday night. You want to know all there is to know about this passion, and you want to share it with the world. You may have even invested your time and energy into sommelier certifications or trips to local vineyards where you've spent hours in underground wine caves learning the details down to the wood grain of the casks.

A dream has been nurtured while you've been pursuing this path: opening your own wine bar. You get beyond the "Could I really?" phase and decide to GO FOR IT. You sit down to write your business plan, and you think, *this should be easy!* because you have it all in your mind: the experience, wines, atmosphere, and memories you'll help people create.

But then you stop. A wine bar means real estate. It means insurance, construction, permits, marketing, loans, and staff. It means a serious amount of cash at a time when everyone is feeling the bite of record inflation. You're not sure you want to sign up for all of that.

Suddenly, this dream is a mountain you can't see yourself climbing— and that hurts, because this passion has become the thing that has inspired and moved you to make shifts, maybe even sacrifices in your life.

The dream doesn't have to die, though. It can simply become. Perhaps the wine bar can start as a private group service, going to

people's houses to offer wine tastings for small parties. Or perhaps it can begin as a "pop-up" in a local store, or as simple as posts about your favorite vineyards on social media.

People who are successful in pursuing their passions have realized a key point: Passions don't need to come to life in a singular way and only for one point in time. Your passion can have many expressions, and each can (and more than likely will) change depending on the chapter of life you find yourself in.

The key is starting where you are and taking the best next step to express the passion you are nurturing. Look at the resources you do have instead of the resources you don't have. Pay attention to the strengths you have inside you versus those you need to build. Look for the support that is waiting for you instead of persuading strangers on day one.

Take Margot Raggett for example. Margot was one of the UK's most successful advertising executives. Back then, she would have told you that she "had it all": the title, travel, and even the expensive handbags! However, Margot experienced a gradual awakening where she realized that the superficiality of the advertising world was no longer for her, despite its rewards and supposed glamor. She began, as she put it, "chasing hobbies" while she was still in her agency role. One of those hobbies was safari travel, and through that, she became interested in wildlife photography.

On one of those trips, Margot witnessed elephant poaching in northern Kenya in 2014. It affected her so deeply that she asked fellow wildlife photographers if they would contribute to a fundraising book. Their response was unanimous, and *Remembering Elephants* by Wildlife Photographers United was published in September

2016, with images donated by sixty-five of the world's top wildlife photographers. Since then, Margot has grown that one book into a full series and has sold more than 53,000 books and distributed more than $1.5 million US dollars to seventy-four different conservation projects in thirty-three countries across Africa, North and South America, Asia, and Europe. Margot was also recently awarded one of the UK's highest honors, the MBE (Member of the British Empire) for Services to International Wildlife Conservation.

Likewise, Junita Flowers didn't start expressing her passion by opening a bakery. She started by blogging for her local library.

"When I started volunteer blogging for James J. Hill Library—which my family thought I was crazy for doing because at that time, I didn't have a job—I built an audience there that came along on my journey starting this business," Junita said. "They encouraged me, and I thought that maybe I should listen to what they were saying. I realized it was bigger than me and that I needed to just do it."

When we break our passion or "the dream" into smaller pieces and match it with our strengths, it becomes possible to keep our promises, follow through on our commitments, and take care of those we love. We don't have to upend our entire lives—we can start right where we are, bringing our closest supporters with us on the journey.

Passion Prompt

* Do you have an idea for a passion that you feel "stuck" on? If so, what is the main reason you are hesitating on it?

* Think of a time when you used your creativity and resourcefulness to solve a challenge. What natural abilities did you call upon?

* Now, think of one way, no matter how small, you could start making progress on your passion. To help, ask yourself:
    * Is there something I can ask people to contribute?
    * What activity might be connected to my passion that I can begin doing freely?

PART THREE:
RISE

When you prioritize your passions, you find yourself standing taller as you trust yourself more with every promise kept and activity tried.

Now that you've explored—and hopefully embraced!—the 12 Sparks, you're ready to continue your journey. This might not mean finding your one perfect passion but, instead, learning to put passion first, weaving it into your life no matter what chapter you find yourself in. I know it sounds big, but that's the point. Living a Passion-First Life isn't always about reaching a destination; it's about choosing, again and again, to embrace what lights you up. When you prioritize your passions, you find yourself standing taller as you trust yourself more with every promise kept and activity tried. You not only *have* a passion, but you also show up *with* passion, energizing and inspiring those around you.

Living a Passion-First Life is not about sudden selfishness or arrogance, nor is it about ignoring your responsibilities or rejecting those you care about. As Alyssa Frank, an events and marketing manager, told me: "I was working all the time because I thought that was my passion. And then I found aerial arts and I've been able to integrate it into my life. Now I have a passion outside of work; I can now set more firm boundaries between work and leisure. And I now work harder in the office because I need to go and 'do my thing' afterwards. It's become like my North Star."

Passions can *transform*, but that doesn't mean that they simply appear. You'll need to consistently take the initiative to live your life, trusting your instincts and acting upon them. The whisper of the voice inside that is nudging you to try that new activity, speak to that person, book that trip, raise your hand . . . you'll need to stop pushing it away and treating it like an inconvenience. That voice is you, and it's telling you to connect back with what you love.

This means that you owe it to yourself to have a plan for nurturing and pursuing whatever passions emerge as life moves forward, with all its uncertainties, responsibilities, and challenges. You will need to consistently show up for yourself so that you can feel how you want to feel and create the impact you crave.

DARE

This journey takes courage—that's why I want you to DARE to move forward, using this framework as your guide:

D: Describe

You have every right to keep your passion private if you prefer. Use it as your oasis of energy that you can tap into whenever you need it.

However, even if your passion is something you can do alone and with no equipment, you'll likely reach a point where you'll need some support. And to successfully get that help, you'll need to explain your passion.

Sharing the precious thing we've claimed as our passion can be intimidating, especially if it's early in our journey. We need support to help our passion flourish, yet we may hesitate to voice our passions for fear of tarnishing them, being judged, or taking up space. These are all understandable reservations, because we want to protect the progress we've made in discovering the passion we now hold dear.

We also know that we can't control other people's responses or approval, or whether we'll let ourselves down by retreating or

unintentionally creating conflict. This can happen with someone who may feel a sense of betrayal or discomfort about a shift in your identity (the identity they have tied themselves to or relied upon), or a change in routine that your passion may require.

That's why creating clarity ahead of any conversation is vital, whether you're sharing with a BFF, a reluctant spouse, or a busy boss. One way to do this is to create a Passion Statement using the following steps:

* Write down the thing that you love (e.g., an activity, an idea, a cause).

* Add context to give substance to the passion.

* Define who your passion helps. This can be you or others (e.g., other humans, animals, buildings, cultures, the climate).

* Articulate the result or hope of your passion to give your statement a foundation, even if that outcome is evolving.

I love to _______________________________________

because I'm passionate about _____________________

so that it helps _________________________________

be/do/create __________________________________.

Here are some examples:

* "I live for fishing! The time alone on my boat helps me reflect on my life and develop skills so that I can be the best father, husband, and leader I can be."

* "I love project management. I'm passionate about making things work better so that our team can live more balanced work and personal lives."

* "I'm passionate about fighting climate change with new technologies like solar energy, because I want to help our children live a life without worry."

The goal is not perfection. It's to create a statement that you're comfortable with sharing and that will invite acceptance or curiosity.

Create and practice your statement as many times as you need to. As you share it with others, notice what questions they ask or what it prompts you to explain. I promise that the more you practice this, the easier it gets. And best of all, your Passion Statement will set you up to ask for help.

A: Ask

Living a Passion-First Life is a fine balance of trusting your instincts, desires, and capabilities, and leaning on those who'll help you along your way.

Want to deepen your meditation practice? You'll need a sign on your door to let your kids know not to disturb you.

Want to join a new committee at work that's outside of your department? You'll need permission from your boss to skip the weekly status meeting.

Want to learn a new style of art? You might need to ask your spouse to pick up your child from school so that you can make it to the class.

These everyday examples can feel intimidating because we're showing vulnerability and, often, part of our identity that has previously remained hidden.

It can feel like retraining our brains to ask for support after years of putting others first. We don't want to add to someone else's day, give them extra tasks, or become a burden to them.

Here's another way to think about it: If you hesitate to ask for help, what would happen if you thought of it, instead, as giving a gift to others?

By asking for support to do what you love, you are giving a "cheat code" to important people in your life. This code gives them a clear way to be of service to you, to help you nurture yourself, and for them to be part of your story. If these people truly love and respect you, they should be ecstatic to receive this new information!

To do this, you'll need to get crystal clear on what you're asking for. If you're not sure what that is, try reflecting on these four categories:

1. **Knowledge:** Does someone have experience that could help your passion thrive? Do they have connections you should know? Or recommendations that could inspire you?

2. **Time:** If you've signed up for a project management class on Thursday nights, that will take a few hours from your week. Who needs to know that? What duties need coverage? What obligations need shifting or delegating?

3. **Money:** Let's say the project management class costs $1,000. How will it be funded? Whose approval do you need? Will that investment create a return?

4. **Encouragement:** What moral support will you benefit from? Is it consistent, tangible, and/or public? Or less so?

Begin by asking one person who has your best interests at heart. Before you speak with them, practice using your Passion Statement so that it flows easily, then make the request. Be open to the outcome, too. If you didn't receive the response you expected, reflect and adjust if you feel it's necessary. And if you *did* get the support you asked for, take heart and continue!

R: Rise

Living a Passion-First Life can often feel like rising. We feel our true identities shine through when we do what we love, even for an hour. We see our strengths rise above our weaknesses, and our spirits will often rise, too, helping to counteract the darker chapters we may experience.

However, there is one emotion that will kill your passion faster than any dismissive friend, busy schedule, or unsupportive spouse: guilt.

As my daughter, Sophia, has grown, I have rediscovered a passion that has forced me to confront my guilt habit—it is my great love

of travel. It started at the age of fourteen, when my parents saved up to send me on a school skiing trip to Italy. It was my first time on a plane, and it lit a fire in me to see the world.

Traveling (especially solo travel) gives me energy and a connectedness to the world. In 2023, I found myself in a crowded, buzzing area of Mexico City, crossing the road with hundreds of locals and tourists. I felt a huge swell rise in my chest, an exhilaration of "letting go" of control of who I was, where I was, and the feeling of being swept along in a current of humanity. I find this sense of freedom thrilling. To wander, to dillydally, to get "lost" are things we avoid in our daily lives. Travel gives them back to us and shows us the treasure they hide.

I have felt the hot flash of guilt as I've booked every trip as a mum who won't be accompanied by her daughter or husband. People have told me how good my husband is to "let me" travel on my own. Friends have even asked who looks after Sophia when I leave her (yes, that old chestnut).

Because I have "felt the guilt and done it anyway," I know now that I'd rather feel guilt for experiencing the thing I love than regret for not trying it. That regret can quickly turn into resentment, which can poison the relationships we hold most dear. I have also learned that once I am traveling, guilt dissipates because I know that I am fueling myself with positive, fulfilling experiences. I'm showing my daughter that my love of travel is part of who I am, and by her seeing me pursue it, she gets to know more of me. She also sees that it's not just allowed but *essential* to step away from daily life to do something that fills us up, and that we are not "less than" because of it.

So, when you're considering investing in your passions but feel held back by guilt, pause. Are you using guilt as a convenient excuse to avoid discomfort? Perhaps you didn't ask for enough support for your passion, so now you feel that you've let people down. Or maybe you're faking guilt because that's what others expect, but if you truly listened to your heart, you'd go after what you want.

Guilt wants to keep us where we are, where society expects us to be. We can hear it, but we need to confront it and then rise—rise above the heaviness, rise beyond the expectations, rise into who we truly are. Sometimes guilt doesn't truly disappear, but when we're brave enough to rise above it, to give ourselves space to breathe and explore, we discover just how high our passions can take us.

E: Evolve

Once you begin to spend real time exploring, identifying, or even pursuing your passions, you'll experience a wonderful sense of momentum, of things finally "clicking." The more you do it, the more you want to do it. But to truly live a Passion-First Life, we need to be ready for our passions to evolve. They'll grow with us, challenge us, and sometimes even transform us into something new.

As Jeff Curtes (a passionate HVAC leader, photographer, and cyclist) told me, "Pivots can keep swinging. If you love something you're not going to pivot away from it, you're just going to pivot into new, better, and different."

Think of passions like the fluffy heads of dandelions, known as pappi—or, as Sophia and I call them, "wishes." In the spring, you'll see fields full of these dandelion "wishes," waiting to fly. When Mother Nature dictates, they take off, often flying hundreds of

miles, helped by their parachute-like structure. Often, there are clouds of them in the sky, waiting to be caught. Sophia and I will cup them in our hands, wishing for something wonderful, and then we'll let them go, blowing them gently to help them on their way.

Our passions are like these wishes—some need to be held gently, while others need to be released to find new ground. Just as it would be impossible to catch and keep every dandelion, we might not be able to hold onto every passion forever. Some will change with the seasons of our lives, taking root in new ways. Others might need to float away entirely, making space for new passions to grow. If that happens, promise me that you'll try not to succumb to shame, guilt, or regret. Instead, stay open to what is ahead of you with the knowledge that, often, our passions don't properly leave us, they simply transform.

Now, I don't mean to imply that passions simply "whoosh" into your life, as pretty as the dandelion scene may be. There is a reality to shaping our passions that many don't want to take on—and that is, as we help our passions find their way, trial and error must become our friends. Evolving the things we love—and becoming more of who we are—means making mistakes, plenty of them. You'll miss a step (or ten), be naive, and perhaps rub people the wrong way with your energy and forward motion. You'll bring too much of yourself at times, go too fast, push too much, or show enthusiasm that others may find hard to reconcile.

When this happens, it can hurt even more than a regular mistake. We can beat ourselves up more than usual and doubt ourselves even more. We love this thing, but how could we not have known? Why didn't we think of making that call? Why didn't we realize this person would feel that way? If you're pursuing a harmonious

passion, however, your integrity is also deepened. Your heart will be in the right place, even if that "right place" turns out to be incomplete or incorrect to others. When (not if) you make a mistake, you'll apologize, explain your intent, and make amends where you can. Remember that you are a good person!

Above all, evolving your passions means learning from the mistakes and committing to growth. If the misstep with your "side hustle" was caused by a gray area of understanding, create a contract next time (and make sure you're protecting yourself). Did the thing you built in your garage over many rainy weekends not work properly? If so, what skills do you need to acquire to improve it? Did someone get upset by a liberty they felt you took with their time? If so, improve your proactive communication for next time. Try to look at your inevitable missteps as signposts for your passions, ones that are helping point the way for you. Above all, do not let the mistake—or the reaction to it—stop your Passion-Seeking journey.

Now, even if we do our best to learn from our mistakes, nurturing our passions can still be plagued by self-doubt so strong that it stops us in our path. This is what I call the "Paula Abdul" effect: Our progress takes two steps forward and two steps back. (I know, I know, Gen X joke alert!)

Here are a few examples:

* You're a passionate baker. Yet you burn the cakes, curdle the custard, and incorrectly measure the flour more times than you can count. And perhaps you think, *Maybe I should get back to mowing the lawn. At least I can't burn that!*

* You sign up for a local golf league after rediscovering it from your twenties. You've been on a winning streak and are loving

everything about being back on the putting green. But during one round, you can't find a hole in eighteen. You leave feeling that you've let yourself and your golf partner down, and you think, *Maybe I wasn't cut out for this?*

* You finally launch that dream side hustle, but you see zero sales despite everyone's support. And so, you wonder, *Maybe I'm the only one who loves this?*

* You join a work committee with excitement, only to face the same politics as those at your day job. So, you find yourself thinking, *Maybe I was stupid to think I could make a difference?*

Inconsistent progress is frustrating precisely because you believe in your passion. When you hit these walls, it's helpful to remember that pursuing your passion doesn't mean pursuing it perfectly. Even tennis legend Roger Federer said during his 2024 commencement speech at Dartmouth College that he only won 54 percent of the points in the 1,526 singles matches in his career. He went on to say, "The truth is, whatever game you play in life, sometimes you're going to lose. A point, a match, a season, a job."

Passion gives us a desire and the strength to get up and try again. There's even a joy in dusting yourself off and proving to the world why you love to do what you do, why you bring something unique to the world. As long as we don't let the mistakes and progress dips run too deep, they can fuel us, giving us experience and stories to inspire others.

Finally, our passions may evolve as we do—what mattered to us in one part of life might show up differently in another. And sometimes, those changes don't always happen instantly, or at the same time.

Take Tracy Moore, for instance. In her twenty-plus-year career as a firefighter, she courageously saved countless lives (and delivered many babies along the way). She also experienced and witnessed discrimination against women firefighters during a career that she was passionate about. When she retired, she wrote a novel, *The Fire She Fights*, about the true stories of over thirty firefighters.

As she said: "Originally, I was going to do individual stories of the women I worked with to try to ensure our stories weren't lost. I didn't know if I would publish or if I would just give a book of their stories to everyone I interviewed. The women I interviewed talked about how it felt to fall through the floor in a fire. Some women cried recalling the last words of a patient they lost. And there were . . . stories of the cruel hazing that went over the line to abuse. I wanted to give the readers that same connection I had while interviewing the firefighters. I felt a novel would provide that—it would allow the reader to go through the whole experience with one or more of my characters. They could see the struggles and at times the failures, but they would also see our successes, our friendships and our lives at home. In a novel, I could also tell the truth without putting the actual women I interviewed in danger and exposing who they were. The novel is fiction, but the stories are real."

If you ask Tracy to describe her passion, she'll respond with "truth and integrity." Firefighting and writing were two different expressions of that for her over time. Her story reminds us to give ourselves grace as we pursue what we love and to avoid the temptation to simply "set it and forget it." Instead, we need to embrace how our passions might need to shift and grow with us.

As you explore, nurture, and build your passions, set aside time to reflect on how your passions should and can evolve. Three questions you can ask yourself are:

144

* How is this passion serving me?

* Do I need to put my passions first more often?

* Does my passion need to fit in differently? Or play a different role in my life?

You may need to adapt, change course, pull back, or push forward. That's all part of the journey. The beautiful thing is that it's entirely up to you. Your passion is for you and you alone, because it IS you.

Even though living a Passion-First Life requires courage, effort, creativity, and regular infusions of belief, I DARE you to try. More importantly, DARE yourself to believe in your abilities, your inner strength, and the generosity of others who want to see you shine.

PART FOUR:
THE PASSION
PROMISE

For your passions to flourish, you'll need to make a promise to yourself—and you'll need to recommit to that promise, over and over again.

In the closing moments of every Passion Collective event or speaking engagement, I give every participant a Passion Collective postcard. Then I ask everyone to write a promise to themselves on the back and add their address on the right-hand side. We mail it back to them so that a few days later, they receive their own promise. It is always the quietest part of what are often high-energy events, as attendees try to capture their desires in a simple line or two.

When you receive that postcard, it's literally a message from yourself, in your own handwriting, from one point in time. It's a powerful reminder; promises can be pinned inside your cube or inserted into a journal. They can even make appearances on your family's fridge.

Here are some that I've been privileged to see:

"I promise that I am going to get back to my confident, creative, incredibly gifted self!"
"Keep speaking your truth. Regardless of the outcome, you did the right thing."
"Your voice deserves to be heard. Use it."
"Ask Pete for coffee."
"I promise to not abandon myself."
"Be a badass!"
"Spend time on my songwriting every day."
"Get the guitar out of the attic!"
"Sign up for that class."
"Go for that promotion. You are ready."
"Paint! This is what keeps you grounded and on the path to healing."

Passion Promises have become an essential ritual for the Passion Collective community. They remind us of the power of promises to add an imprint inside of us—an encouragement, a reminder that we are worth it. They inspire us to honor that "buzz" we are looking to create.

Following through on our passions can depend on our schedule, our health, and our tolerance for discipline and self-management. When we do, it can feel good. As a result, we build confidence in ourselves, and we begin to trust and rely on ourselves more. When we don't, we may shrug and chalk it up to a busy week, or we may begin to blame ourselves for never staying on track.

We make promises to many people and systems in our lives. We promise our spouse that we'll love them, for better or worse. When I became a US citizen, I promised to abide by the Constitution. As a Girl or Boy Scout, we'll say, "I promise I will do my best. . ." Every year at work, we set our annual goals, which are promises to pursue goals so that we can all be successful. Even when we sign up for a gym, it's a type of promise; we're promising ourselves the prospect of good health. In all these cases, there is an external entity we are promising to, even if it's invisible.

Rarely do we make a promise to ourselves. Sure, we can write down a list of goals or habits we want to take on, but a promise is different. A promise honors our innate worth, our goodness, and the confidence in ourselves to do the thing.

For your passions to flourish, you'll need to make a promise to yourself—and you'll need to recommit it, over and over again. Your promise can be a starting point—it doesn't need you to remortgage your house or go full *Eat, Pray, Love*. It can be a simple, straightforward action you commit to, so that you can begin, or continue to live, a Passion-First Life. Keep it actionable, but don't shy away from feeling a little audacious when you write it. What feeling do you truly wish for? What are you willing to do to get it? What does Future You want you to do next?

Your Passion Promise

CUT HERE

Born to Buzz

Your Final Passion Prompt

1. Reflect on the promise you want to make to yourself.

2. Write your promise in the postcard. (It's OK to write in your books, by the way—just don't be that person who marks up a library book!)

3. Open your phone and create a recurring reminder or to-do task for your Passion Promise. Add the promise, a date, and a time you want to accomplish it by. Then, add an alert to remind you one week and one day before it is due.

4. When the Passion Promise is done, check it off!

5. Repeat.

ONE LAST
WORD

The power is in what you gain.

You may have started this book skeptical about what "passions" could bring to your life. I get it, it's not always easy to put ourselves first. And yes, we've all heard that life is a journey, not a destination—which can feel hollow when we're facing challenges or haven't reached the goals we've set for ourselves.

Our passions take time to rediscover, and they transform as we do. Often, the thought of carving out time for something that lights us up—in a way that only we understand—can feel so far out of reach that we simply wait. Maybe we've been told that the things we love aren't valuable enough. We bury our passions deep or crush them before they have a chance to grow. Why? Because pursuing what we love means becoming who we truly are. It means living a life we know we want more of.

A Passion-First Life asks us to surrender to forces we may not fully understand, to release the grip on obligations and expectations we've put on ourselves. We need to accept that what we love is part of who we are, even if that doesn't match the identity we've spent years building or how others see us. We must challenge the assumption that the daily grind is just "the way it is," that we should suck it up for the next five, ten, fifteen years until retirement.

This isn't about dropping our responsibilities. It's about removing the armor we've worn for so long. (Harmonious passions need openness and trust—armor has no place there.) Sometimes it means redirecting time, energy, or resources that have gone elsewhere for years. None of this is easy. This journey demands work, courage, openness, resilience, determination, and, often, plenty of laughter!

Here's what I have learned: the power is in what you *gain*.

With every practice completed, every meeting held, every mentee helped, every stroke painted, or every note sung, you are fostering the thing you love. You are adding beauty, joy, creativity, and fulfillment back into yourself, and you're reminding yourself of who you are, what you were BORN with—your strength, your magic, your beauty.

You begin to realize that if you step away for an hour, the people who matter will love you even more when they see you shine. When you live your life this way, other people notice. They'll be proud of you *during* this journey, inspired by the "buzz" you create in yourself and others.

You'll see that your one action, even if it's a shaky "first draft" or kick of the ball, is beginning a domino effect—a chain reaction that inspires, connects, and motivates others to reclaim their strength and uniqueness.

A Passion-First Life is rarely all unicorns and cupcakes. (If it is, tell me where and when, and I'll be right over!) But know that it is worth every investment you can make into it.

Choose to do more of what you love. FIGHT for it.

You have one life. Do all you can to *truly* live it!

REFERENCES

Introduction

We have never been more disengaged from our work, from Tera Allas and Marino Mugayar-Baldocchi, "The Hidden Costs of Quiet Quitting, Quantified," February 28, 2024, https://www.mckinsey .com/uk/our-insights/the-mckinsey-uk-blog/the-hidden-costs -of-quiet-quitting-quantified.

. . . the happiness of young people has dramatically declined compared to later generations, from John F. Heliwell, Richard Layard, Jeffrey D. Sachs, Jan-Emmanuel De Neve, Lara B. Aknin, and Shun Wang, World Happiness Report 2024, Gallup, 2024.

. . . and women report being unhappier now than in 1996, from Betsey Stevenson and Justin Wolfers, "The Paradox of Declining Female Happiness," National Bureau of Economic Research, 2009, https://www.nber.org/papers/w14969.

The world is in turmoil, from Helion and Company, "Conflicts," https://www.helion.co.uk/periods/21stcentury .php?sid=24b5a14e426544c3d5f7896ded9aece1.

Part One: Grounding

"Nothing great in this world has ever been accomplished," attributed to Georg Wilhelm Friedrich Hegel.

"Reason is, and ought only to be, the slave of the passions and can never pretend to any other office than to serve and obey them," from David Hume, *A Treatise of Human Nature*, 1739.

List of emotions, from Alan S. Cowen and Dacher Keltner, "Self-report captures 27 distinct categories of emotion bridged by continuous gradients," *Proceedings of the National Academy of Sciences (PNAS)*, September 5, 2017, https://www.pnas.org/doi/10.1073/pnas.1702247114.

Note that passion isn't on that list, from American Psychological Association, "Emotions," accessed December 2024, https://www.apa.org/topics/emotions.

Then, I found the work of Robert J. Vallerand and his colleagues, from Robert Vallerand, *The Psychology of Passion*: A Dualistic Model, Oxford University Press, 2015.

Vallerand and his colleagues didn't just stop with their helpful definition, from Vallerand, *The Psychology of Passion*.

A study commissioned by Fisherman's Friend, from Scarlette Matthews, "What's in a Friend?", Richmond & Towers, October 5, 2022, https://rtc.london/making-friends/.

"The last of the American dreamers," from "Titan Pilot Is a Booster of Deep-Sea Tourism," *New York Times*, Daniel Victor, June 20, 2023, https://www.nytimes.com/2023/06/20/us/titan-pilot-stockton-rush.html.

"Cherished a shared passion for adventure," from "Shahzada Dawood, Executive, 48, and Son, 19, Die Aboard Submersible," *New York Times*, June 22, 2023, updated June 26, 2023.

"My view is that these are all calculated risks and are well understood before we start," from "A Global Reach in Business Jet Brokerage," *Business Aviation Magazine*, September 2022, 21.

Take, for example, Lee Meyer from Nebraska, from "US Driver Pulled Over with Huge African Bull Riding Shotgun in Car," *The Guardian,* August 31, 2023, https://www.theguardian.com /us-news/2023/aug/31/bull-car-riding-shotgun-nebraska-watusi.

In 1985, sociologist Robert N. Bellah and his colleagues defined three different ways that Americans viewed their work, from Robert N. Bellah, Richard Madsen, William M. Sullivan, Ann Swidler, and Steven M. Tipton, *Habits of the Heart,* Harper & Row, 1985.

. . . a minority see their work as a "calling," from Justin M. Berg, Adam M. Grant, and Victoria Johnson, "When Callings Are Calling: Crafting Work and Leisure in Pursuit of Unanswered Occupational Callings," *Organizational Science* 21, no. 5 (2010): 973.

"What If All I Want Is a Mediocre Life?", from Krista O'Reilly-Davi-Digui, July 31, 2020, https://www.alifeinprogress.ca /want-mediocre-life/.

. . . it's been scientifically proven that pursuing harmonious passions helps with our self-esteem, from Vallerand, *The Psychology of Passion,* 186–328.

There's a reason why the energy drink market is expected to grow to $240 billion by 2027, from Statista, March 15, 2024, https://www .statista.com/topics/10313/energy-drinks-worldwide/#topicOverview.

And, as academics have proven, pursuing our passions promotes growth, from Vallerand, *The Psychology of Passion,* 186–328.

Part Two: Sparks

"People gave me the stupid advice," from Evan Carmichael, "STOP Asking Yourself THIS STUPID QUESTION! | Simon Sinek | #Entspresso," posted by Morning Motivation / Evan Carmichael, April 16, 2020, YouTube, 12:21, https://www .youtube.com/watch?v=8eq0AUafvo8.

. . . following your passion "not only fails to describe how most people end up with compelling careers but for many people, it can make things worse," from Cal Newport, *So Good They Can't Ignore You: Why Skills Trump Passion in the Quest for Work You Love,* Piatkus Books, 2012.

Mark Manson bluntly tells us to "Screw Finding Your Passion," from Mark Manson, "Screw Finding Your Passion," accessed December 2024, https://markmanson.net/screw-finding-your-passion.

Spark #2: We Know What We Want

A recent study at the Mauritshuis Museum in The Hague, from "Girl with a Pearl Earring Visually Captivates the Viewer: Mauritshuis Presents Results of Neuro Research," Mauritshuis, October 2, 2024, https://www.mauritshuis.nl/en/press-releases/girl-with-a -pearl-earring-visually-captivates-the-viewer/.

. . . if we focus on the positive emotions that Barbara Fredrickson says, from Barbara Fredrickson, "What Good Are Positive Emotions?",

Review of General Psychology (1998): https://pmc.ncbi.nlm.nih
.gov/articles/PMC3156001/.

Spark #3: We Ignore Labels

Identity is both, as the American Psychological Association tells us,
definition from American Psychological Association, APA
Dictionary of Psychology, updated April 19, 2018, accessed
December 2024, https://dictionary.apa.org/identity.

Three different dimensions, from William James, *Principles of
Psychology*, 1890 (reprinted 1950).

Spark #4: We Refuse to Be Controlled by Comfort

*Extrinsic motivation typically involves engaging in behaviors that
give us "external incentive to engage in a specific activity,"* definition
from American Psychological Association, updated April 19, 2018,
https://dictionary.apa.org/extrinsic-motivation.

*Intrinsic motivation should be our friend, but it's by far the less
practiced of the two, especially in our lives outside of work*, definition
from American Psychological Association, updated April 19, 2018,
https://dictionary.apa.org/intrinsic-motivation.

See Greg McGee's art on his Facebook page: @mcgee.greg.

Spark #5: We Fuel Ourselves

*In 2007, a study by economist Alan Krueger claimed that we're
only spending 20 percent of our time on things that are meaningful
to us,* from David B. Krueger, "Are We Having More Fun Yet?

Categorizing and Evaluating Changes in Time Allocation,"
Brookings Papers on Economic Activity, no. 2 (2007): 193–217,
https://www.brookings.edu/wp-content/uploads/2007/09/2007b
_bpea_krueger.pdf.

*In 2023, the US Surgeon General declared a new public health
epidemic: loneliness*, from PBS Newshour, May 2, 2023, https://
www.pbs.org/newshour/health/loneliness-poses-health-risks-as
-deadly-as-smoking-u-s-surgeon-general-says.

Spark #8: We Craft Our Jobs

A first step is job crafting, from Amy Wrzesniewski, Nicholas
LoBuglio, Jane E. Dutton, and Justin M. Berg, "Job Crafting and
Cultivating Positive Meaning and Identity in Work," *Advances in
Positive Organizational Psychology*, Volume 1, 281–302.

. . . to "(be) an obedient child, going with what my parents influenced,
from Astrid Benedetto, "Transform Your Career," September 29,
2023, in *Passion Chats*, produced by Laura Best, MP3 audio, 25:31,
https://www.buzzsprout.com/1150286/episodes/13253509
-transform-your-career-with-us-bank-dei-leader-astrid
-benedetto.

Spark #10: We Proudly Dabble

*What we've lost—and what we need to regain—is what expert Todd
Kashdan calls joyous exploration*, from Todd Kashdan, "What Are
the Five Dimensions of Curiosity?", Medium, January 4, 2018,
https://toddkashdan.medium.com/what-are-the-five-dimensions
-of-curiosity-7de73684d53a.

Its official definition is, definition from Merriam-Webster, last updated April 27, 2025, https://www.merriam-webster.com/dictionary/dabbling.

. . . I prefer the more casual definition, alternative definition from Online Etymology Dictionary, accessed December 2024, https://www.etymonline.com/word/dabble.

Spark #11: We Reach Back to Move Forward

When Junita Flowers found herself in a situation marred by domestic violence, from "Harnessing Hope: How Baking Helped Junita Flowers Rise to Help Survivors of Domestic Abuse," Passion Collective, May 5, 2021, https://www.passioncollective.co/blog/harnessing-hope-how-baking-helped-junita-flowers-rise-to-help-survivors-of-domestic-abuse.

Spark #12: We Are Relentlessly Resourceful

Take Margot Raggett for example, from "Out of Africa—How Remembering Wildlife Led Margot Raggett to Rediscover Herself," Passion Collective, June 16, 2020, https://www.passioncollective.co/blog/margot-raggett.

Likewise, Junita Flowers didn't start expressing her passion by opening a bakery, from "Harnessing Hope."

Part Three: Rise

Here's another way to think about it: If you hesitate to ask for help, this concept is found in *The Art of Asking* by Amanda Palmer, Grand Central Publishing, 2014.

As Jeff Curtes (a passionate HVAC leader, photographer, and cyclist) told me, from Jeff Curtes, "Find the Yes," August 1, 2024, in *Passion Chats*, produced by Laura Best, MP3 audio, 34:26, https://www.buzzsprout.com/1150286/episodes/15435387-find-the-yes-with-jeff-curtes-hvac-leader.

Even tennis legend Roger Federer said, from Roger Federer, "2024 Commencement Address by Roger Federer at Dartmouth," posted by Dartmouth, June 9, 2024, YouTube, 25:03, https://www.youtube.com/watch?v=pqWUuYTcG-o.

Take Tracy Moore, for instance, from "The Fire Within: Tracy Moore Shines the Spotlight on Female Firefighters," Passion Collective, August 2, 2021, https://www.passioncollective.co/blog/tracy-moore.

THANK YOU

Firstly, thank you to the Passion Collective community, thousands of you worldwide who have come on this journey with me and trusted me with your stories, hopes, and dreams. To the Passionados who supported my first events, the strangers who've responded to my emails, and the businesses who have brought me into their organizations, thank you for helping me create this space.

To the team at Wise Ink, especially Amy, Hanna, and Lindsay, for helping me make this book a reality!

To those who have given me opportunities to grow as I "made my own path," especially the Right Reverend Stephen Lake, Loretta Ahmed, and Jim Wolford.

To my circle, those who are always there for me—especially Liz ("You have something to say!"), Mari, Erin D., Kristi, Tina, Doug, Adam, Sal, Sarah Z., Kiki, and my "Firm" crew.

To Brian, who knew that "Titanic" would take us so far?! Your steady advice, support, and true friendship means the world.

To David, thank you for all you have done and all you do to love and support us.

Stuart and Joe—thanks for cheering me on!

To my grandma and hero, Marian Ferguson. Your strength, independence, and support helped me lay the foundation to the life I now live.

To my beautiful mum, Linda. A few sentences cannot sum up how much I love you and rely on your true, constant love and support. Thank you for letting me go, so that I could create a life in America. I love you always.

To my daughter, Sophia, for giving me the gift of being your mum. Work hard for what you love, follow your heart to make your own path—you deserve all that is beautiful in this world.

And finally, thank you to my husband, Graeme, for letting me be me and for working so hard to give me space to do what I love. Most of all, thank you for reminding me that "you have more power than you realize." I will carry that, and your love, with me always.

ABOUT LAURA BEST

Laura Best is the force behind Passion Collective, a global community redefining the way we think about work and life. Growing up in Dorset, UK, she followed what seemed like the "right" path by studying history at the University of Warwick. During her time there, a summer adventure involving a hair dryer and a Greyhound bus (long story!) led her to Minneapolis, where she fell in love with the city's creative energy and possibilities.

After Warwick, Laura built a PR career in the UK, working on award-winning campaigns, like Land Rover's "In Search of a Legend" and NSPCC's "Full Stop" (which sought to eliminate child abuse). At twenty-six, she left the UK to join the Minneapolis advertising scene, armed with just a suitcase, $500, and her snowboard. In the following years, she became known as one of the Twin Cities' top digital marketing leaders, working with brands such as American Express and Target.

In 2014, Laura launched Passion Collective, initially as a women's community, to create space for real conversations about passion, identity, and fulfillment at a time when many didn't feel they had the

permission to support each other or voice their needs. Since then, she has awarded microgrants to Passion Seekers across Europe, the US, and Africa, launched the *Passion Chats* podcast, and spoken to thousands of leaders of all genders across the US, sharing practical ways to do more of what they love in work and life.

Laura's relatability, humor, and belief in "Practical Inspiration" resonates deeply with audiences because she knows their journey— she's experienced burnout (and risen from it), been the "only" at decision-making tables, and felt the loneliness of being an ambitious working parent far from home.

"We have one life—are we truly living it?" This question drives Laura's work. Her mission is simple: help people bring more of what they love into their lives, right where they are. Because when we embrace our passions, we light up our own lives and inspire others to do the same.

Meet Laura at: www.passioncollective.co

"Laura Best (is) incredibly kind, professional, prompt, and genuine. Her presentation was incredibly impactful to women and allies alike. She not only gave an engaging and insightful presentation . . . but she left everyone with actionable steps after the session concluded. Laura is professional and, most importantly, authentic, and it shines in every way she communicates and holds herself. The world needs more of her light!"

—Jessica, finance leader

"I attribute my drive to identify passion in my work to Laura Best and her work with Passion Collective."

—Alex, IT leader

"'What lights us up?' Laura Best challenged us to explore the depths of our passions. We've all experienced those moments when our hearts beat faster, fueled by something we deeply care about. Laura's words resonated, urging us to understand why certain things ignite our enthusiasm. If your organization seeks to ignite teams and foster inspiration, I wholeheartedly recommend tapping into Laura's talents."

—HeeSook, nonprofit board member

"Laura Best encouraged us to reconnect with our passions and make promises to ourselves to prioritize them, even amidst our busy schedules. It's all too easy to lose sight of what truly lights us up, even when we seemingly 'have it all.' Laura's message resonated deeply as she introduced the concept of harmonious passion activities that align with our lives and bring us joy."

—Meritas

NOTES

Use this section to reflect and jot down your notes. I've also included a larger version of the exercise from Spark #11: "We Reach Back to Move Forward." Feel free to reproduce this as many times as you need to on your journey.

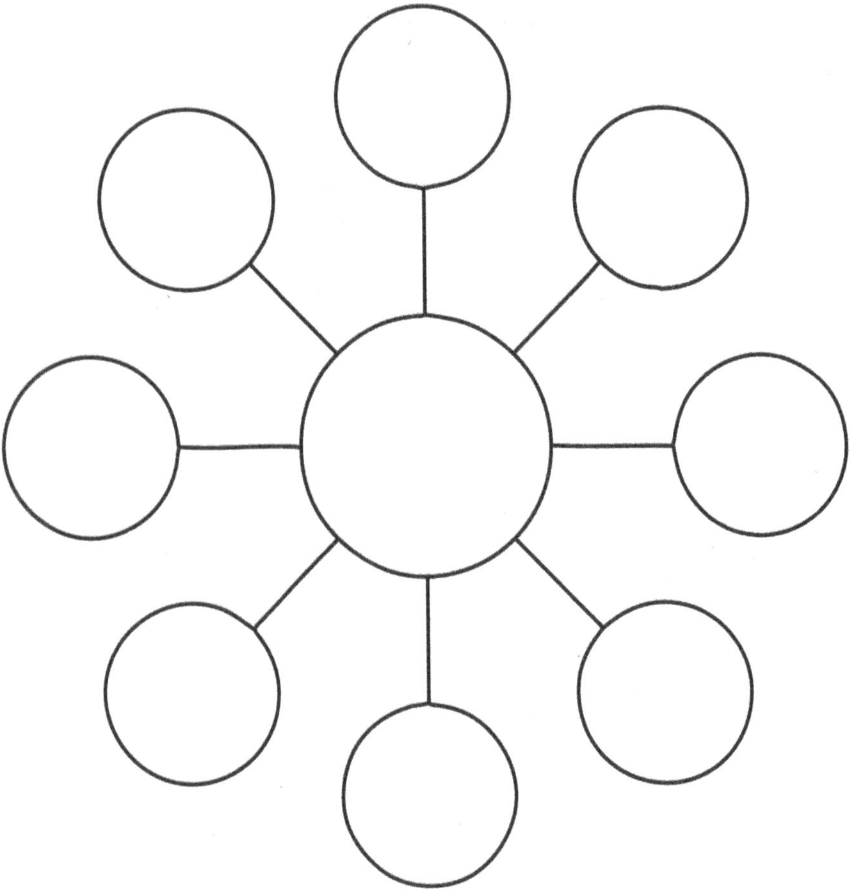